ROCK SALT & GLISSANDOS

Rock Salt & Glissandos

Steve Fisher

the synæsthesia press
Tempe, Arizona

© 2001 by the estate of Steve Fisher. All rights reserved. No part of this book may be reproduced in any form or by any electronic or mechanical means, including information storage and retrieval systems, without permission in writing from the publisher, except by a reviewer who may quote brief passages in a review.

Some of these stories and poems first appeared in *TriQuarterly, Pearl, Shenandoah, Ironwood, Chiron Review, Witness, Epoch, Iowa Review, Gypsy* and *Between C&D*.

First Edition

The characters and events in this book are fictitious. Any similarity to real persons, living or dead, is coincidental and was not intended by the author.

Library of Congress Cataloging-in-Publication Data

Fisher, Steve
  Rock salt & glissandos/Steve Fisher
    p. cm.
  ISBN 0-9652505-6-3 (pbk. : alk. paper)
  1. Southwestern States Literary collections.
  I. Title
  II. Title: Rock salt and glissandos.
  PS3556.I81435R63 1999
  818'-5409 — dc21   99-31-1 CIP

Published by
the synæsthesia press
P.O. Box 1763
Tempe, AZ 85280-1763
www.chapbooks.org

Printed in the Unites States of America.

For Cherry,
because Steve would have wanted it

&

briefly for bruce

*When I'm dead,
fucker, and
the speaker playing
Beefhart
goes:*

    LUSH GARDENS ABOVE

from a favorite tune:

*watch, bud,
as my lips move;
my head
hot & bright the
   way
we've always clenched lobes,
   negotiating
that high-key BARK.*

table of contents

foreword i
taco mask 1
the first few hours, alone after prison 11
bio on judge cunt 13
late afternoon 15
underdose 16
a laggard in blood-red love 26
controlled populations 29
one for an over-worked mantor 31
soap line 33
a quick ugly dream between luxury hards 40
skull monkeys 42
basic pharmacy 45
variations on the robe 47
frenching spanish for cherry jean 62
weather nose 63
slam 64
monocraft 65
short steps to another world 73
pitchfork standing flame & time crap filaments 74
slowtime in the jailhouse 76
electric latches 77
ball-peen thrush 92
dysphoria 94
boosted dream poem 96
cactus fish 97
cooking film 120
responding to prison guards 121
methods of exile 122
somewhere there's a coffin with a soft blue lining 130
thermal hibernation 131
windy gray 133
my friends are the next generation of ants 146
hang over use in pharmacopia 148
whorl 151
tightening the rings on the sun with my forehead 163
ugly and multiple 165
such pittance, the thoughts 166
blockades 167

Rock Salt & Glissandos

foreword

To refresh my memory for the writing of this piece, I visited the Special Collections of the California State University, Long Beach Library where a thick stack of Steve's letters to me are housed. A number of things about the very first letter, dated May 9, 1984, struck me as significant. He was already suffering from a number of the types of ailments that were to make it hard for him to stay off drugs: an infected eye, dental problems, a lymph node recently removed. He had been playing a lot of pool, a game at which he was apparently a shark. Knowing that I had spent my three years of graduate school in Tucson, 1961–64, and loved the place, he brought me up to date on various locales: the dog track, the Miracle Mile, the Green Dolphin tavern. He mentioned having played hockey in Detroit as a kid. He was sending work to a mutual editor, Belinda Subraman, at *Gypsy*. Mainly, he expressed himself in what was already a vivid, original, figurative prose style. It didn't take a Maxwell Perkins to spot that he had both talent—maybe genius—and material. And that, as in Edmund Wilson's classic study, *The Wound and the Bow*, his abilities were doomed to co-existence with endangering traits. He concluded (ominously, in retrospect), "But for now I'm gonna dig into my pills and go to sleep."

We were to correspond regularly until shortly before his death a decade later. His letters were as extraordinary as his stories, less disciplined but even more spontaneous. I decided early on that he was the best writer of prison life and of the drug world that I had ever read. He wouldn't have liked such pigeonholing, but it is high praise indeed. He didn't get to write as much as, say, Burroughs, but I would in all honesty rather read Steve. He never sacrificed to postmodern trendiness the reportorial authority and stylistic inscaping of a Hemingway. In life he sometimes had to shuck and jive, as the marginalized must if they are to survive (and it forced me at times to be on my guard with him), but in his fiction he sought the truth—about the systems that entrapped and ultimately crushed him, and, with more difficulty, about himself. He celebrated life's moments of intensity, of Joycean aesthetic stasis, and he delineated the skills required to negotiate survival in an infernal world of which few of us, knock on wood, will ever have direct experience.

Steve Fisher

These elements of his brilliance are on display in classic stories such as "Taco Mask," "Soap Line," "Cactus Fish," "Windy Gray," and "Whorl." Possessing such abilities is one thing, though; having the heart to pursue a literary career in the face of overwhelming obstacles is another. Steve often lacked things most writers take for granted: adequate paper and pencils, decent lighting, privacy, minimal comfort. Legal battles were a constant. So was pain. Addiction was a fact of life. Aloneness was part of the writer's condition. He was not the sort of "artist" who has nothing better to worry about than "writer's block." His blocks were solid and bruising. It is a miracle that he wrote anything; a greater one that he got work into print. The greatest miracle is that he managed to produce this substantial body of work of sustained excellence. And I truly feel that he would have considered the publication of this volume the culminating event of his life.

He was fortunate in his editors—Jim Camp and those whose periodicals are credited here—and, eventually, he enjoyed an Indian Summer of love and encouragement with the poet Cherry Jean Vasconcellos, whom he met at a Bisbee poetry festival and who has been instrumental in ushering his work into posthumous publication, here and in *TriQuarterly*. It truly is a small world after all. I had known Cherry since 1964 when I lived in an apartment in Alhambra beneath the apartment of her brother. Maybe our worlds are structured, as Pythagoras and Buckminster Fuller might have suspected, according to some hidden law of triangulation.

I hope this volume will not be the end of Steve's story, but the beginning. These works belong in the anthologies. The young have much to learn from him about writing and about life. We all do. Foucault and others instruct us that it is only through the understanding of worlds such as Steve's that we can come to an honest understanding of our own. I know that Steve (whom I only met once, at the Reno Room bar in Long Beach, near the end of his life when he was frail but undaunted) was a major presence in my life. A friend through the age-old epistolary medium. I hope that his letters to me and others will someday be published—the opportunity awaits some enterprising scholar. I hope the critical attention will begin. I wanted very badly for him to survive and to succeed. The former proved impossible, but this volume constitutes a cornerstone of the only immortality that mattered to Steve Fisher. I believe his words will live on, as Auden put it, "in the guts of the living."

Gerald Locklin
California State University, Long Beach
Spring 2000

Rock Salt & Glissandos

taco mask

There was trade off the alley, and the cars moved slowly in the street, inching into the all-night market. It was a short little utility street in downtown Phoenix that dead-ended about fifty yards from the DOG run in Alhambra, which was the main classification prison in the state, the one everybody was sent to once they finally picked up their time from the judge. It was about midnight, on a Sunday in July, and Willie watched them from his upper bunk, mostly as a distraction from the ten others in his cell. The five years he had received for "attempted possession of narcotics" was nothing to think about, except in legal terms, which he would do once he was moved to a camp, so he rather drifted away from the stories for a while, rolled Republic institutional, watching his fingertips stain yellow as he smoked. Through the grating and scratched glass he saw the people drink freely from their bottles and cans. Oh yeah? he thought passively. Well, somebody's certain. But it was more than a simple street party, he was beginning to realize, and started feeling the weight off the road as if it were a movie he was in. He could tell what was going on. It came easy, and to most city people before any first fix. Floyd, on the other side of the walls, also knew as much. He was a matter of transaction, balking at the gauntlet which Willie laid idly into his dome . . .

Even though the temperature was still around 100 degrees out, the only ones who seemed to be nervous or sweating were those who hadn't yet scored: heroin, mainly; that black Mexican chiva. The lot was crawling with it, this lone Circle K, and Floyd knew he'd have to make the trip down there soon: his heart beat hard and wild to one side, above his weight, as his central impulses skittered upon wires of flesh. His head felt replaced by something that felt like an outstretched octopus. He had money, enough for an eighth of a gram, but he didn't like the feeling of exposure and possible police carney that came with these public thresholds. Especially when right across from the prison. But the choice was to get down there or suffer the unbearable lower heavens in his second-story room. He slipped his pointed shoes on, along with a thin sleeved shirt. Already he felt chilly.

A barking commotion came through the hallway as he squinted to lock his door. Frayed sounds from the end of a coiled tube seamed the stagnant air, filling it with yaks and safari. Midnight, and the sound of mother and child. A child screaming for something to sleep on as mother prepared to toil the night. The night was her rope ladder, but Floyd always kept a few paces from nudging her trail of business. He walked down the hall toward the stairs, tilting his skull against the two open and relentless ends. Already the others in his house burned darkly into the night.

The mother's flesh hung awkwardly on her bones, and her mouth worked open in one corner. Floyd thought she might have been a compensation add-on from a factory accident—five-hundred pound skivs, and forklifts with peeling dirty yellow paint roared and crashed through his mind — but her name was simply Dot, and as the kid quieted into his passing eyes she said, more crazy than militantly, "See, women are superior to men. Just look how Dale comes with me."

Dale only looked like he would learn to fight soon, getting young licks off on his mother.

"I suppose so," said Floyd, "but probably only if you are one."

"Tie your shoe right this time," she hollered at the kid.

Floyd leaned into the stairwell cautiously. He felt as if he were walking on cotton balls, going down the steps, everything hesitant and unsure. But he finally made it through the door, closing the squall behind him.

The light on the street looked tired, somehow sagging like an old cloth. Even the bugs weren't attracted. A few telephone poles down the road looked like giant pencils that wanted to walk away. The sidewalk was patch-worn and cleric, so Floyd walked through the deserted street as the silence hummed, eyeing the light from the Book of 3 bar. In a neighborhood receding from ultimate activity, the Book of 3 glowed orange and red and yellow infinity. It *moved* on this side port of deposit. It was life and music and variegated snow.

The lights burned an image that rather caught on a sort of inner retina. He looked away, down to where he walked, to the shadows that seemed like pit drops, and just might be. He felt the oil in his short, thin hair, then slowly ran a hand up his forearm as his head sprinkled coolly with impulses. He clipped along, anxious of pulse, his lungs full of batter. It had been a long twelve hours since his last shot, but he was only a few thankful minutes from the K.

And it was a sudden sight, a gloss, welcomed with a cold length. The people mingled in huddles for a while, then broke into packs and teamed with the night. Ten or twelve groups formed continuously, while the drunk and aimless circled with laughter, snorting lines from cut-boards they brought in.

Around the hem of the lot stood party fragments: pocked faces and broken teeth in gravel-coated neon, lightly stepping to the movement of rap . . . that apparently was a thrust downward, starting with the chin. Glass and rags ringed the area, along with a stinking pile of oily parts that terraced a section to their deep side, just next to a three-story building which crumbled on the adjacent plot. They were robbers, boosters, hold-up and quick-scamming men, women, working the variable con. With dealers, dope fiends, half-heads and three-for-one markdowns of one total fashion: physical futures who hustled an advantage, checking into the Kingdom while the wind laid low. A rather beachfront Christian even wove through the mob, speaking of sin, of redemption, of conversion to hysterics. And all but the beachfront were quick to react with one single opinion: the jobs they were working were temporary. They were simply part of a well-planned national statistic, prospering tonight through low negotiation.

Floyd was at the edge of his skin, working his way through the crowd. He looked around until he saw an obvious contact, a tall black guy in a dark red T-shirt, taking money from a shorter, black woman, her skin an orange underdress. Floyd was white. It made no difference. What did make a difference was the looming prison across the street, and the cringing flow of open dealing. And the Phoenix police, with tactics that frequently overlooked the laws they were supposed to enforce. This wasn't New York, and it just seemed preposterous to do business this way, to be set in such shallow margins with no outs. He thought a demented cartoonist could probably draw it and get the caption right. But it made him tighten and wince, thinking next time Bermudez, his main source, was going on a Tucson run, he'd cover his ass and avoid it all. Maybe even clean out a bit, if necessary and possible, but most likely just stockpile, or shoot low.

As he walked up, the man turned slightly, as if expecting him.

"You lookin' to get high, my man?"

"Tar," said Floyd, "I need a piece of Tootsie Roll."

"How much you need?"

"Can you do an eight ball?"

"Whatever you want," he said, handing Floyd the dope and eyeing him.

Floyd peeled the foil off, looked at it, then felt for thickness in the cellophane. It felt something like two matches, pressed together, and almost as long. It was black and shined like glass. He put it under his nose and breathed slowly, slowly through the corkboard and mucus, and picked up a light floral opium. Yes, he thought, this would do fine, and right off the street. If I have to do junk now, at least I'm close enough to Sonora to get good stuff.

"How much?" he asked. The price was almost always sixty bucks on the street. But it would get him through the night, and open his eyes in the morning.

"Sixty," said the dealer. "You want it?"

"You have some clean works? With sealed caps?"

"I got some new ones. Only been used once."

"No way," he said. "AIDS. I can give you fifty-five."

"It's sixty, and you can bleach the 'fit."

Floyd tried a quick response, lost, paid the sixty and stuck the dope in his change pocket. His eye caught the enamel sheen of the Circle K, and he noticed business being conducted through a small window. The whole of it glared like a paste-up to him, like something artificial taught in kindergarten with a pointer stick: an illuminated cutout on a black easel. It made him sick to think about it, and he wanted to split, but as he moved in that direction there stood the street Jesus, book open, Bible lame. A thick, puffy, five-inch scar that ran down one side of his skull, lit like a pig's pink ass, told Floyd this guy would be dangerous with intent. The Jesus stepped just a hair to the right, locking into Floyd's path. Goddamn, he thought, now this fucker's gonna try and mat me with a prayer.

"God WILL redeem you, brother! Open your soul to Jesus now and HE WILL HAVE YOU!"

"LORD, NO!" said Floyd, and a number of horns began honking as if they were pipe-neck birds. Screams and yelling; the flash of lights and the heavy musk of exhaust flagging over. A lone, brute-piercing wail of womanhood, followed with a masculine "YOU'LL FIND THAT GAP BETWEEN YOUR TEETH PACKED WITH DIRT!" and then a window being smashed in a car. People looked over, moving, to see if there was something to get in on. That's simply the way it worked. Floyd felt his gut flush hollow with nerves, and saw the dollar sign from an old-fashioned cash register as he looked out of reflex.

"AND YOU AIN'T NEVER TO COME BACK! NEVER TO COME BACK BUT TO SOME OTHER DAMN FOOL!"

"STOP IT!" she yelled. "LEAVE OFF THIS MINUTE 'FO YO' FACE FILL WITH GLASS!!!"

The tires screamed rubber but the car merely bobbled. You could hear fists pounding on the roof, strong hands, before it finally caught pavement and sped off. It was amazing there wasn't an accident. But Floyd wasn't thinking about that. The streak that bore through him would have said: I know too well what's happening down here. It's rough enough just answering the phone, without having to circulate and watch people do it.

"Now, there's a couple who make sense."

It was Blossom, a sort of ex-hippie who had drifted around for years, not wanting anything, not needing very much, who landed in Phoenix when he found how difficult it was to simply live as himself without the common American ornaments. He still wore tie-dyes and lived light, hitting the streets as a matter of course. Floyd knew him from somewhere: maybe his friend Risa, the pouchmaker? They stood together, watching the high-fives, elbow butts and so forth at curbside, but Floyd only wanted to get going. His head was like a can of pineapple rings that were separating.

"What happened to your thing about love?" Floyd asked, but he could barely think straight, much less put himself, or others, into workable terms.

"That might have been an example of it," said Blossom. He then added, "I'm starting to open up a little more."

"I'm starting to open up as well," said Floyd. "I'm getting the hell out of here."

He didn't really even look at Blossom. His eyes just darted around, fixing abstract forms into a loose mold of darkness.

"I'm on my way to the B-3," said Blossom, as they both began moving off. "I've got to meet Holly. Have a beer or something with us. She may have some dilaudid."

"All right," said Floyd, stepping around a shank, evil-looking bastard, fairly dreading the Book of 3 at this point, but thinking of Holly and the dilaudid. He didn't like the idea of slamming junk in the B-3 head, but like all addicts he couldn't refuse a free fix—if Holly had it. But it had worked out before with her, so Floyd was attracted to the lure.

"You got a smoke?" asked Blossom.

He pulled out a couple of Camel filters and gave one to Blossom. His lips were dry; wrinkled like cigarette paper. When he lit up and inhaled, he saw his ribs etched in like horizontal bars. He gagged and coughed at the same time. Got a headache. Took longer strides, which Blossom matched. They walked the five minutes to the bar, smoking, mainly Blossom talking.

But it's what they didn't see that caught a special tier in Willie's mind. About the same time he saw Blossom and Floyd walk off, he noticed a late-model Ford sedan, moving slowly, rather understated for its make: AM antenna, sparse molding, blackwalls with those solid, bulb hubcaps—all factory-issue. And there were two younger guys—bearded, mock dudes riding in it, paying less attention to the gathering and commotion than they were, apparently, to one specific individual—at least that's what Willie thought, the way their heads worked in tandem. He thought they were cops, undercover cops who were up to something, and he wasn't alone: one of his Mexican cellmates, who was looking out the other window, suddenly sat up and said, "Narco." The others hopped off their bunks and crowded around the two windows, tilting their heads in order to deep-focus through the narrow glass. There was no need for any of them to ask who was who or what was what.

The deal went down on their side, unobstructed, as if it were staged. One of the dealers went over to the driver, bent down and talked a moment, then straightened up and looked around, easy of motion. He was big, black; buffed like those traffic cops who hang out in the gym. He pulled from his crotch a manila envelope that was folded with creases just about the height of currency. The Homeboys smelled it. They knew. They began laughing as he handed it to the driver. Before the car even drove off, they partied.

"Whew baby, those be some *long* duckets."

"Must be five grand; five grand to rents that space."
"We had that going down in Excelsior. Cost us ten grand a month!"
"*Mucho feria, ése.*"

They were sweating in their orange jump suits, Willie and the nine others, excited about the professional conduct they'd witnessed. It was only good business, they argued, to operate on efficient policy. They scuffed around the cell, drinking from the sink, talking, until one of them went into a long, morale-boosting speech, outlining the methods he'd used to move large amounts of cocaine, how to cook pounds into rocks, and the principles of the "double-up" technique. Then there were cars, women, houses, neighborhoods, all, he said, the result of hard work. Everyone settled on the edge of their bunks, listening closely, as the cell became a sort of conference room full of wistful associates. Even a few street cigarettes—tailors, they were called—were lit up and passed around. Willie listened along, glancing from the window to laugh, going with the flow of energy—which was a sort of bulkhead release, but not really too bad. It was a needed lift for all: a respite from the smell, the overhead asbestos, the dull swampy lighting and initial prison uncertainties. They kicked it like that, as individuals rather than slateboard, burning the reserve from the filament in their bones. Just where the hell is the rest of America, in the middle of a Sunday night? thought Willie.

Right away there was further contraction. Not that the bar was particularly hostile or restricting—it was about as open as bars get, for that matter—it was simply Floyd's reaction while horribly sick to a confined space of public gathering. His shirt was touched with sweat. His eyes were bloodshot, hanging from veins like fried eggs in their sockets. His sense of balance modulated, refusing to focus or center. And, worst of all, he thought that everybody knew what the problem was and would somehow turn it against him—right then, before he could do anything about it. Then he told himself that they all probably came in sick—sick, hung over, trembling and limb-taut from alcohol poisoning. It didn't help much, since it was hardly a matter of psyching up, but it gave him something to play with while Blossom found Holly; while he made it to the bathroom without spilling into the waitress and customers. He was somewhat surprised to make it. Groaning into those peaks of drunken noise, he thought, had really helped to do the trick.

But they only had a small restroom, and the door was locked. He stood under a very yellow bulb that lit up the storage hall he waited in, listening to more than watching a game of pool just in front of him. God, those balls cracked so loud he thought a fan was blowing out his ear, whipping the sound through his head like that. The jukebox sang, the old oak register tallied and the ice machine dropped a load. Madness madness who's this fucker in the head? His works and the rest of this kit itched in his sock. When the door finally opened and the fucker stepped out, walking away, he felt a great sense of relief in the overall down-bearing upon him.

He got in and worked quickly, running the water and spreading his things out. There was a short ledge behind him, which he laid his spoon and syringe on. The place was small, but he finally had a sense of being alone. It was a good feeling, and it worked with the anticipation he had when he pulled out the *chiva*. He smelled it again, then cut it in half, pressed it into the spoon and yanked. There was a soap dispenser. He washed up good, got the point, then palmed a handful of water. He drew the water up and eased it into the spoon. When he got it into the plunger, he pushed the commode door open and sat on the john. He heard the juke box bass beating into the stall like a wrecking ball against the hull of an ocean liner.

He put it in a vein on the side of his wrist, booting it once. His eyes staggered, then warmed up and closed gently. Windows opened all around him, in him, to pastoral pockets of space. He saw it bleaching his body coloring — like tracer fluid through an illuminated man. He felt his toes, his kneecaps, his shoulder blades. He moved his arm and felt his shirt touch lightly. His thoughts returned to steady cadence, blessedly ethereal as they were at the moment. He began to feel whole, reconnected, and totally on top of his game. He wanted to laugh at the insanity of circumstances, but he simply smiled and rubbed his nose. One hell of a life, he'd often thought, and he was glad at the moment to be part of it. If he stopped to consider the scheme of things, what was coming besides the next shot, he wouldn't have felt too bad because he could only be in one spot with one brain, thinking. That usually worked the magic for him, when given an opening. What a fine place Earth could be, if you only went with the spin of the throw! Even in the men's crapper of a neighborhood bar.

He rinsed his works out and packed up, listening through the wall and the air vent to Stevie Nicks. She reached into him, touching points of his body that were beyond explanation, never sounding better. Oh *yeah*, he thought, bending in half to shake his hair out like a wet dog. Then somebody began pulling and knocking on the door. Before he opened it and went out, he paused to feel himself, all in one piece, directly in line with the spheres.

Blossom was with Holly, at a small booth away from the door. A picture of Boojum Shorty and a saguaro growing out of the dust were painted on the wall behind them. A hanging lamp made from cactus ribs hung above the table, barely lighting up Holly's girlish freckled face. Ah, she looks sweet, thought Floyd — how'd she ever become a dope fiend? Their eyes met between dancers and she smiled — good sign, good sign! He flashed a finger to say he'd be right over, then stepped up to the bar for something sweet. He grabbed an open stool at mid-rail, next to an older gutty man with a white whisk-cut. A knickering. There was a bowl of salsa and some chips. The guy motioned to them.

"Eat up, partner. Wha'cha drinking?"

Floyd didn't really want any chips, so he just looked ahead and said, "Ginger ale and milk, with an egg blended in."

Steve Fisher

The old gut was drunk and couldn't understand, and became somewhat incredulous.

"Ginger ale and milk? *Play's at first! Play's at first!*"

Floyd felt a shorter second rush flow through. God, how sweetly our earth grows! Why must this be illegal? Then he said, "Well, my gut's been on the thin side lately. Thought I oughta stoke it, rather than stretch it."

"You're in the honor seat, partner, what'chu want's on me tonight. This being the anniversary of Sally's departure an' all. Go ahead and have a chip. Say, it's great for a bum stove."

Well fuck, thought Floyd, dipping one anyway—"To Sally," he said.

"To Sally!" said the old gut. "Best horse I ever rode, back in my ranching days."

"And now you've retired to bar whiskey?" asked Floyd.

"Naw, I'm just here on a little business."

The salsa was incredibly hot, and Floyd spun around and spit it out. But the fumes bled through his face anyway, fitting him, he thought, like a taco mask. He looked up to see the bartender.

"Bring him a beer," said the gut, "one of your best. Old Milwaukee on draft!"

"That's the best?" asked Floyd.

"Sir, I stand at the front of my race on that. Go ahead—for Sally."

To hell with fantasy, thought Floyd, if it means his train of thought, even though he was slightly amused. He then told the barkeep, "Ginger ale and milk, with a little nutmeg blended in."

"Aw shit," said the gut, disgusted because he'd have to drink alone. "Bring me another beer, an' a shota that Scotch."

"Coming up, gentlemen," said the bartender, walking off to make them. Floyd pulled out a smoke, feeling calm, feeling the worlds between them and the differences in addictions. He wished neither on anyone, but felt glad he could inject his, rather than sit around the bar like that, drinking it. But he'd also reached the conclusion, from earlier, heavy turns of wine, that drinking only tightened his environment. At least during this stretch, he'd try and leave it alone.

The bartender returned with the drinks, set them down and collected his money. Floyd left a small tip as he got up.

"So you really are gonna drink that?"

"And maybe for breakfast, too."

"Play's at first!" he growled again.

Floyd laughed this time as he crossed the floor, skirting the flare of dancers. He straightened his back and inhaled deeply, his nose free of gristle and sandpack. But the place was filled with smoke and he coughed in caricature. Holly saw him coming and pressed closer to Blossom, making room for him in their booth. "I've got a few d's for you, Floyd," she said as he sat down. "May God lick lightly your neck," he told her, then reached into her long red hair and did it himself.

He took a slow drink as Holly began talking, mostly of mutual friends—Randy, Lilly, Loraine, Chuy—while Blossom daydreamed at the table. These were people she and Blossom knew from the streets, people he had met maybe once or twice but never hung out with. He enjoyed her voice more than anything, and lay against her while she talked, the bar working below them. She was hot with young warmth, cushioning his head as he smiled from an easy plane. And the drink in his hand felt cool and refreshing. He drifted along until a kind of balance downshifted, returning him to common meter, then got up to stretch his ass. He flexed the cords in his legs, gazed through the smoke at the pool table, then dropped down across from them and asked Holly for the dilaudid. He was ready to leave.

Diminuendo.

Holly fiddled in her purse for a moment, peering around the room as Blossom sucked at his beer. You might say they had no way of knowing, but Holly shouldn't have just passed the stuff to Floyd over the table like that, with all those people in the bar. The undercover cops who were stationed there, sipping wine coolers and mimicking the regulars, got to Floyd and forked his wrist on the table before he even had a chance to toss the shit onto the dance floor. One stood at Floyd like a shadow block, while his partner sealed Holly and Blossom in the booth. "Open your hand, motherfucker, before it gets broke," he told Floyd rather softly, as if it were a racing tip he wanted no one else to hear. He had his badge flipped out in Floyd's face.

Floyd opened his hand. Three tiny yellow pills were in his palm, which was lined so red from the cop's grip you could practically read his chart from the swivel bar. The other cop plucked them out like he was picking through birdseed, drawling to his partner, "Looks like a controlled substance to me; it sure as hell don't look like bus fare." A third cop came up with a radio and stayed at the booth as Floyd was led to a corner and handcuffed. They wanted to dump Holly's purse on the table, but a number of people had semicircled the area, and they couldn't be sure what their reactions would be. Holly and Blossom weren't handcuffed until they were out front, but they were separated right away. Floyd was led out last. He stood under a blue light to the side of the place, next to some prickly pear and other cactus, feeling the July heat work at his beard. He was certain the heat had something to do with the way his whiskers were growing. His chin itched with hot, wet stubs, but his hands were behind his back. He let it go.

Their rights had been read, but no one was talking. Even Holly, who still carried an air of innocence about her, knew enough to wait until she got a lawyer. Seventy-two hours, even in jail, going through all the conditions, was a safer bet than any form of self-admission, regardless of what the cops said. But they didn't listen at the Book very long, because four cruisers pulled up in a matter of minutes, three of them running their squad lights. Floyd winked at Holly before his head was pushed into the rear seat. He wasn't able to see her as she winked back.

"Looky here, Holmes, she may go to selling her story in the back of that cruiser 'fore charges even be writ. I knows a young woman; I can be *knowing* thangs!"

"She has looked young, now hasn't she? But you see all that red hair? She may be tougher than we think. Almost look like a horse-woman from here, god*damn*."

"Hahaha."

"Yeah, she may be up to some heart—an' probably jus' for a few joints, anyways. But that about sticks to my shorts, the way they be doin' her."

"I hear ya."

"And that one dude, you can tell he be doing some hea*vy* hair-on."

"I'm telling you, Holmes."

"I'll just be warming up my bunk for him, right *now*."

They were moving away from the window, thinking romantically of the old times and pre-prison situations. And why not? There was death in the ceiling and the floor was nothing but concrete—that surely wasn't going to sustain them, but something had to. Willie was interested but detached, and decided to brush his teeth. Then maybe in a few hours he'd be able to sleep, but it almost wasn't worth it: corridor scenes mixed with wire cages and termination exits seemed only to ball up and smear through his brain like wadded newspapers. Then, after a couple of hours, he'd awaken again. But cold, like refrigerated.

One of his cellmates looked at him at the sink:

"That bar was just the wrong place. Where they should have been was up here at the K, hanging out in the light with the heavy cheese. *Never* been busted 'round that kinda money."

He said it right, but was almost looking for some kind of assurance of himself.

Willie said, "Yeah, we've got a fine Constitution, if you can afford it," then listened to the laughter as he worked on his teeth. He wasn't going to let them get his teeth as well. "Anybody know what's for breakfast?"

The air went plump for a moment, then noise rolled like normal from down the row. He looked into the mirror by mistake, and squinted at his reflection.

"Tomorrow's country gravy over biscuits," he heard someone say.

the first few hours, alone after prison

I come back & here's the old place

womanized (I mean the old girl sweethearting) all along

& all the old *things*:
thoroughly grazed with dust frostings & anchored
 with root forms
from long ago, at least a year—

 it's longer than you may think
& at least a year longer through *stricture* alone—

yet (paradoxically) it's as if I could'a merely gone, left
 & come back
from a weekend retreat
 or a quick
skin-session with a fantasy named Marsha
 or a deep
butterfield, imploding with woodwinds,
except for the way stillness & stencil
 have settled my environs
400 notches beneath today's optic stretch—

 this is simply time without clench,
common attrition, a yellowing—
 there's just
no life snapped with ginger
or garlic or chili or cayenne,
 no wasp dens
here, no flex . . .
but plenty of old muscle
as I abruptly left it—like a battlefield
 dimmed at dusk: raw, forefucked turf, decarcerating now—
an old army of music, books, razor frenetic modal ideas, corner
 weapons & concepts

Steve Fisher

on a span of sleepy fishnod calm,
   sheltered (bless her)
& ready for my next world of allegro, theirs too . . .

But the old place is alright & I'm damned lucky
it's even here. I've learned
   from my trainers
the poetics of maintaining access
   & thank them now personally
as I glance down the breezeway
   at 3 a.m. foliage
      72 degrees in Tucson February
without the pressure of light—

I thank them with silence, the way I was taught—

   this gentle spoke

      of color & grace
      of portal divinity
      & tactical rapture

as I sit here tonight
   relaxed
   in tight

with the bloodflow of creators & criminals.

Rock Salt & Glissandos

bio on judge cunt

The courtroom is paneling
tan paneling
that's all except a flag,
and the hidden sound
tiles sponging
the attorneys' objections.

Judge Cunt, at the bench,
believes strongly,
passionately,
in the commitments of her appointers,
she thinks up to them

not across to the accused

she bows to power
and sucks.

Her forehead, it's noted,
resembles a snare drum
and her language is regulated

   pre-managed
   selected

by the enemy
her voice is a sharp
cheese through the grater.

It weaves to the defendant

   stringy,
   elastic:

"Five years"

Steve Fisher

first offense
probation is what he's unwittingly been

living.

But she communicates well,
effectively
    with children
    with legal briefs
    the founded
    the arranged
    the people,

however,
stand miffed, confused.
"I'm an impartial justice"
she will tell you
or anyone,
but consider her opinion
is defined by the legal

text.

Like her discretion, morals, compassion
and the like:

    it's a trick-bag in a windtrap
    something in her blood

it collects down there
la-bãs
in the pantyliner

    her attitude
    isn't bad
    but her atmosphere

is.

late afternoon

Lazy cigarette
smoke over concrete
soft from chilly
rain
5 convicts
claiming the world
a shower
next Tuesday —

Steve Fisher

underdose

Lotus stood in his boxer shorts pulling a towel through his hands one evening, a darkened cloth of sunlight buttering his blond-haired corn-cut as the dorm filled with shadows and noise. He showered as always at head count, while the rest of us played cards and bought what we could with cigarettes. Then he opened his locker for a stock check, pulling out pencils, old magazines, half-tubes of shaving cream and mismatched boots from a collection. I noticed a round sort of grin jerk over him, but it was more like a spasm in a face gone wild with prison dentistry. He was only about twenty four years old.

The peculiar adjunct to Lotus were these rock-bottom locker items. He was a yard supplier of general goods—fine merchandise and cloth—yet nothing on hand appeared more than a remnant: a milk carton, a candy wrapper, a one-eared pair of sunglasses, the lenses scratched and stained.

Or a container of generic baby oil, speckled with dirt and sweat. This was not the quality—and certainly not the product—that you'd expect from someone in his line, which included fresh fruit and Levi's, and personalized stationery in your choice of four colors. Hypodermics were scarce but available, and needn't always be special ordered. I wondered why he had no more of a showcase than a high-fashion shoeman who would wear only guard boots.

But I knew that some years back (through a directive out of his control) he was put on Sinequan, and the theory was that this drug pushed up on your brain, jamming it into the fore of your skull. This might explain the agitated chop in his rhythm the same way surgically altered lungs, leaving half a tight breath, would affect a bar rocker's performance. It was entirely possible that he disbanded through this therapy, that there was nothing of use to him and no way it would matter.

Rock Salt & Glissandos

I thought quickly of this as I lay on my cot, watching him scarecrow around. If there was nothing he needed but the void of camaraderie, prison was as fine a place as any for him to stretch out and run through his cycles. Still, there was a return on his goods that went somewhere for something. I had no idea what it could be.

He ambled toward me in an atrophied clip-step that had something to do with his lima-bean kneecap: the one cap was small and never locked into step, and the leg bowed as if taut like a flexing rod. But the motion of his arm was robotic, jabbing the air as he came closer to me.

It's just an impediment, I thought. I'll suggest something if he gets too close to my cot.

I could do things with reason, even with Lotus. I kept thinking that it explained why I always had problems with the half-grades down in the probation department, even though it took fourteen months for them to violate my probation and send me to prison. I was only a drinker, caught up in the courts after receiving faulty medical advice about a drunkard's liver.

As Lotus came up through the dorm din I clasped my hands to my chest, church-style. In one hand he had a bag that he opened, passing it under my eyes. I saw razor blades, two bananas, a can of Pepsi and neatly folded pin-ups, surely the latest from a selection of men's magazines. He gestured with a finger-v to his lips, asking for a cigarette. That's one habit a drug-packed brain will never cure.

I reached under a drawer in my locker and pulled out two Camel filters. Lotus reached in the bag and came up with a fold out, then stood like a wall mount with her picture before me. She was fine, all over, especially this clamp of flesh that would turn me to an idiot if only there were five true minutes in this three-hundred-world lifetime. I noticed that the upper right corner was dog-eared.

"This slut's been making it all over the yard," I said. "You can do better by me than to pimp paper."

A wrinkle crossed his lips as he returned her to the bag. I handed over a Camel and reached for a banana. It was bright, fresh, chilled and intact. I stored it away for later.

"I'm in the market for color," I told Lotus, toying with a match as I lit it. "Color like pictures and designs, like a fire truck parked in a sunset, or a blue glider landing in a butterscotch field. Something that will jar the gray light from my eyes, 'cause that's all I look at all day."

I poked the match at his smoke, then lit mine as well. We inhaled as rap music careened off the slick white walls. Suddenly, the dorm flooded with corridor fluorescence. My eyes snapped on like a three-way Mazda as I jerked and adjusted to this institutional night beat.

"I can get you a mural of war, or a skydiver smoking a joint," he said with incision, his body perfectly still.

I thought for a moment, then said, "Bring me the diver. Long as there's no

Budweiser parachute."

He dropped the bag on my bed and clicked his shoulders like a gracious storekeeper, thankful your purchase has been his one item that just wouldn't move. Then his elbows came up and his index fingers joined like an x.

"No deal if there is, but here's what I want if there isn't," he said.

He told me what he wanted and why, his sharp voice paved with nicotine. My ears warmed with blood as I listened. A window unlatched nearby and a breeze off the yard blew over us like a small wave.

It seems three years ago—just prior to his incarceration—Lotus and a sister named Sandi were coming home from a party in a stolen car, a friend named Kurt at the wheel. The cops gave chase at some point, and Kurt veered down an old dirt pass that quickly became a rock-strewn off-shoulder of Highway #5, Benson, Arizona. The Plymouth bounded fast through this outstretch, almost sailing like an airdrop into a wall of hard earth. All three were injured, but Sandi suffered a severe hip fracture that prevented her from walking again. Lotus lost most of his kneecap, some of his shin and couldn't walk for nine months, but only he and Kurt received felony charges and prison time to kill. Sandi got a misdemeanor pandering fine, and as a result of her handicap now drew money from a government fund. It was less than she had made as a small-time file secretary at $6.25 an hour, but then her standard of living had changed dramatically.

Lotus stood over me at the foot of my cot, a dark, dancing fluorescence engulfing his head. He felt that money was available to him as well, but didn't know how much, or where it would come from. He knew it would be the government, but who exactly were they? If he could establish a "handicapped" status he would apply for small business loans and special grants; these would be used to set up a modest store where he'd make keys in the rear while his sister, up front, sold office mottos and Day Glo posters and souvenir clocks to the yawbacks off the streets. He would also be eligible for hardship release—a strategy within his plan—exchanging three prison years due for a term of parole.

There was a remote possibility for this to happen, I thought, and all he wanted was an initial letter, explaining who he was, which he would send to a lawyer that his sister had heard could work miracles in "gray law"—which in his case were weakly defined sub-sections of invalid statutes that the lawyer would work with a specially applied language, evoking a judgment the bench couldn't deny. All Lotus knew—or cared about—was this chance to get a slice of the pie. Then he would settle in the palm of a back room, grinding out keys as his belly got fat. How the lawyer would be paid was something I didn't ask, though I imagined it to be a contingency-type thing.

"Why don't you write the letter yourself?" I asked him.

I didn't mind *buying* his stuff with cigarettes or effortless forms of exchange, but a letter was too much like work. I knew, however, that a crucial half-step of cognizance that would allow him to write a letter *down* on the

Rock Salt & Glissandos

paper was now held in check in his brain like a redline-security field. It was an aphasic condition I described as gravel burns to the frontal lobe, and it rarely affected his speech. But he'd never make the mail without someone's assistance.

"'Cause this is a business deal. Your letter for my poster."

"You'll have to do better than that," I told him. "You'll have to mitigate me with a week's worth of fruit and uh . . . two Pepsis"

"You're talking crazy now. I'll give you the fruit and the poster for the letter. Deal?"

"All right, deal."

I could sympathize with his situation and the fact that he wanted to get ahead. I often thought that the best way for me to succeed on parole was by winning a lawsuit and becoming a person who *offers* work of some sort, not as a person who must go to work daily, crossing so many Main Streets in 5 p.m. rush hours, potentially a felony in each step of travel. Then after parole I'd take a year off—for vitamin boosters, poetry and the sensual.

But the deal was set: I'd have the letter for him in the morning. He'd supply his own stamp and envelope, but I had to address the envelope for him. Considerate of this small afterthought he loaned Emily, the debauched pin-up, to me for a week.

After evening head count cleared, around 6:43, the dorm emptied out and I began working on the letter. It wouldn't take much, of course; more of a note saying, "Look, I'm writing for Homeboy here, a young man who sustained multiple injuries—permanent damage, of course—while riding in a stolen Plymouth. His gross motor control is so impaired that he has problems walking at times, and when he does get around he quakes and attracts nothing but catcalls and stares. It's a wonder he can move at all, and when he gets on the streets again I'm afraid he'll have nothing but trouble with prospective employers and the police—unless, of course, he's protected by competent counsel who will *demand* that a financial stipend be provided him from the appropriate government source. With the fine record you have in these matters we've decided that you, and your staff, are the sort of people we can entrust with this claim. I also suggest you ask him about the accident, because the Plymouth bottomed-out during an endurance performance and the company might be liable for negligence and wrongful injury no matter who the car belonged to at the time. You might want to check his prison records too and see why he was administered Sinequan, the heavy Thorazine-like antipsychotic, after his accident. (The profound effects of this drug are one of the reasons he can't write to you personally!) He may be in prison but that's no excuse for malpractice—as you well know. Besides, he's a car thief, not a sociopath. Sincerely, Lotus & Fiduciary."

I'd give Lotus the letter and point out the possible suits he and his new lawyer would have to think about. This would be worth something to me, perhaps a shirt or—if I explained it slowly enough for him to completely

19

understand—an administrative-type favor somewhere down the line. I approved of the methods this attorney would use on behalf of a person like Lotus; I signed the letter which now only awaited his signature and addressed the envelope, thinking of a tough motherfucker who would help him; just a claimant who suffered moderate symptoms of yard senility and needed some type of support in order to better provide for his sister.

I dropped the letter into my locker, then pushed in the upside-down drawer that I used as a desk top. I peeled the banana and ate it right down, then closed up my house—my locker, my wardrobe, my outfit, my *rack*—with a Master lock. I'd go out on the yard and maybe get into a game of Ping-Pong, or lift weights for a while in the gym. Later, after lockdown, I'd look at the letter and correct obvious spelling errors.

Maybe Lotus would get a shot of the big world in sunshine.

I stepped through a dirty pink swab of corridor light, then down my dorm wing to the heavy footing of a prison yard in darkness cut with floodlights.

Five minutes later I was at the softball field, sitting in the bleachers with Stark Hodger. He and Lotus were partners at the prison, but he had recently made parole and would serve less than ninteen months on a four-year sentence. Parole was mainly a technical perimeter which kept the prisons full, but Stark added ideas and overdrive to his release proposal and would be out within a month. Hope was really work tempered with little disciplines. We all stood a chance.

The fans (the inmates) hollered as the Smugglers played the Banditos in a mid-season drive for first place in our compound league. The Smugglers had added some new infield to their lineup, franchising three young hitters from Hector Varella's training camp, all high-priced rookies who brought at least two cases of soda apiece. But the Banditos had an unending roster of Mexicans—a solid card of muscle and henchmen—organized by *jefes* into the league's top contenders. They had a 9-3 lead now, at the top of the second, with Tommy Salazar due up at the plate.

Stark was chewing popcorn as I sat down beside him. He passed the bag over, a brown stream of mucous shooting from his mouth. I took the bag and mentioned Lotus to him, that his time might be short since he now would retain counsel—"a fantastic lawyer who was hell with the code book."

"I thought he just had a wife who screwed all the prosecutors," Stark said. "But maybe I'm thinking of somebody else. Yeah," he said, "could be. Lotus have any street backing?"

"His sister, and probably his parents."

"His parents are dead." Stark punched a moth as it flew by. "All the better," I said. "He's trying to make it on a hardship release."

Salazar cracked a drive straight back to the pitcher. It was a play which the Banditos practiced, since fisticuffs on the field would automatically expel any player. The shot caught the pitcher in the shoulder near the arm joint, and he spun around, dropping to his knee. The fans roared for Salazar, even after the

Smuggler recovered and threw him out at first base. The warden appreciated a club that triumphed by the rules.

"Appeal first base!" someone shouted.

"The punk pulled his foot off the bag!" another yelled.

Lotus suddenly spoke from behind us.

"Bad call at first?"

"Usual bullshit," Stark said, looking ahead. "Heard you might be getting out."

"*Yeah* I am. I'm just about *outa* here," Lotus pronounced as if apexed.

"You can make it," Stark told him. "No big deal."

"It's always a big deal," I said. I handed Lotus the popcorn.

"Course it is," Stark said confidently. "I just mean if you got a lawyer and backing, you can practically be out the door."

"I know I'll get out," said Lotus, biting down on a wad of corn. "My sister's got me a lawyer."

"Well, it sure helps to have your case re-examined," I said. "Six years is a long time for a Plymouth."

"You ain't a-kidding, Bud. They gave me time for a BMW."

"Tell him what you're gonna do when you get out," I said.

"Take care of my sister," he told Stark, then looked at me. "But he knows all about it."

"She's a good girl," Stark said. "She'll make the difference."

"I wanna find a real doctor that can fix my leg. That's what I wanna do."

"You mean they can fix it?" I asked.

"Maybe," he said. "I didn't see a real doctor, just some jail doctor."

"They *might* have been able to fix it," Stark froze into bleakness. "Probably too late for that now."

"But at least I'll be able to find out, least I'll be able to know."

One of the Banditos hit a long drive over the right fielder's head; "Ya burned him!" some of the fans yelled. Two runs scored but there was a close call at the plate: the batter contended that he was safe, but the inmate-ump called him out. A guard stepped on the field amongst boos and catcalls. The ump's decision was final. It was a call that would be disputed and settled after the game, without affecting the box scores. Joe and Vin and the network leagues only thought they set the final standards.

"Ah, this bullshit!" said Stark. "Out by an arm!"

"Yeah he was," said Lotus, balling up the popcorn bag, then squashing it with his foot. I had seen enough and got up to leave. Real bats were nipping into the light atop the pole at first base. They lived up there, these peculiar dog face bats; we lived up there with them. When one flew into our dorm by mistake one night, the question was, was it intentional?

"Time for me to look for some Ping-Pong," I told them. "Catch you guys later."

As I headed down the third-base line for the gym it dawned on me that

Steve Fisher

Lotus had had three seventy-two hour home passes in the last two years, all without incident. This was important testimony to his worthiness, demonstrating for the record an ability to be something other than crime prone. Lotus certainly deserved a chance to be with his sister, and the more I thought about it the more Stark's comment about lawyers and backing—to get you out the gate—made sense. Lotus was a good candidate in theory, and we could only wait and find out what the lawyer would do with the basics.

When I peeked in the back door of the gym I saw a handful of Indians playing cards at a table, but no Ping-Pong players. The floor shone and the tube lamps burned but the crowd was elsewhere, mostly at the game.

I headed on the walkway back to Crook in the hot night. The inmates at the ballfield howled as another play was made, their voices gusting over the solid, flat compound. I decided to take a quick shower, then catch up on my correspondence. Maybe I could find something on my little headset radio as well. The water adjusted and I stepped into the shower, the only inmate from our dorm to bathe at that time. Again, the action was elsewhere. I took a deep breath and noticed a smoker's ulcer in my throat, a Camel burn that felt like a shiny aluminum shield. It came and it went and there was nothing I could do about it: the prison doctors were far too violent to trust with anything as sensitive and important as a windpipe. I splashed in the water for a few minutes, than lathered up.

Air was the thing that counted most. Without a suck of the big sky you would forever lose reason. Your tactile perceptions would give out without air, a scrub of dead skin left hanging from your sides. Your tongue would not taste and your eyes would squirt pus. Your head would swell up with a feeling of sweatsocks: damp, secreting a chill like ammonia on cloth. Your organic sensibilities were rankled without air—fresh air from the clouds and the soil—and it needn't be forest-pure.

It was important to get the sun on you, too. It brought the blood to your skin and worked with the air as you pulled it into your lungs. It opened you up with a vibrant drive, promoting mental health. It was one of the keys to successful confinement, getting a little bit of sun from the yard each day. Without the right mixture of sunshine and air you would soon stiffen up and go off.

I began drinking coffee, as an oxygen substitute, back in your county jail. I seldom drank it before that, but after three weeks of no air, and very little food, I turned to coffee to help find a pulse, drinking a re-brew or rinse that was hell on the gut. It got my head moving when there was nothing, nothing but the walls, or the wank of probation officers, who rarefied into a low-level drizzle. The coffee was good with the creamer, and I developed a habit of five cups a day.

I was busy with my thoughts and the right light to judge them as the morning sun broke the east. Sixty of us lived in Crook dorm, which was now quiet with sleeping felons. Homey brought me a cup of Folgers, which I fixed with non-dairy creamer and sugar. A sort of wren or a jay was barking on a fence as I sipped the coffee and lit up a Camel. I'd been smoking forever. It took the rest of the cotton and spears from my head.

Lotus smoked, too, as I showed him the letter. He was in blue jeans, white T-shirt and his own pair of state boots.

"You've really got the possibility of lawsuits as well," I told him. "At least one, 'cause of the Sinequan. But it's up to you to remind this guy, to push him in that direction. Understand?"

"*Yeah*, I understand," he said with a smile, his words spitting out like arrows. "I'll get it all that they'll have coming to me."

"Good. Don't let them give you the rod."

The rod was the most frequent thing to come. It came in countless forms and varieties.

"Uh-uh!"

I gave him my pen and he scrawled out his name on the letter. It was a line like a mountain range drawn way down in scale. I picked it up from my desk and folded it, then stuck it in the envelope.

"Lick it," I told him, "and don't forget a stamp."

He licked the letter and dropped it on my "desk," flattening out the crease with the palm of his hand. A stamp came from nowhere and he licked that too, then placed it on the top right-hand corner. The ball of his fist came down like a capping machine, sealing the stamp with a quick flick of his wrist. He was gone then, on his way to the mailbox, sculpting a future which he held now in hope, his small broken buttocks folding in on him like wings. We could expect a reply in four to eight weeks.

I drained my coffee and set out into the morning. It was bright and cool, and the air felt fine as it rushed to my brain.

Three weeks later I was just hanging around, scratching my ass as I read the bulletin board near the library. A loud gang of blacks—stretch rodents, we called them—were congregating nearby, outdoing each other with their own version of street trivia. I recognized a few of them as motherfuckers I beat regularly at Ping-Pong, a game I now excelled at thanks to the new used pair of tennis shoes that Lotus had given for my mention of lawsuits. They were stolen, no doubt, but tampered with and adulterated beyond identification.

I cut for the yard office in something of a power walk. I could see that the mail list had been posted, so I paced myself over, avoiding that first fist of crowd. I had drunk to be alone, and now I finally wasn't. But despite obvious prison laws, such as overcrowding, I could usually sidestep a nucleus population (like the one at the mail list) through my indifference toward the stride of mass-media pursuits.

The mail list was a Xerox of the master population sheet. It was a dull gray copy, flecked with spots that the copyist never bothered to clean from the glass. Next to Lotus' name was the letter L for legal mail. Next to mine was an open grid. I walked back to Crook, wondering how this lawyer would perceive the situation. Then for some reason I thought of pheasant hunting back in Ohio as a kid, of those cold gray afternoons with the shotgun and the boots and my old man, routing out birds, but mainly just exploring.

Lotus came back with the letter, marked C. M. Jovine, P.C., on the return address. We opened it at his house, and he listened on his bed as I read it out loud. "Dear Lotus," Jovine began,

> Thank you for your letter. For me to evaluate your potential claim, I will need to see your prison records and your medical records. Also, I'll need a copy of the accident report and medical findings as per the accident. To that end I have enclosed several release forms for you to sign. I'll also need your social security number and your date of birth. I will help you if I can, but please be aware that many other people also want help, and we only represent about one-eighth of the people we talk to.
>
> Sincerely,
> C. M. Jovine

The sun came into Lotus' house and I could see the letter clearly. Jesus, I read into Jovine's short-arm technique right off. I read that Lotus wouldn't be a member of Jovine's elite one-eighth, and that he probably had a low rung of ugliness if we persisted after he rejected the findings of our claim. And there was Lotus, a lifetime away from me, sitting on his old, rusty bed.

"Perfectly ambiguous," I told him, trying to smile. "We get these authorizations signed and send them back to Jovine. He'll look at your records and begin working on your case."

Lotus smiled, then eagerly broke into an exhausting gait, like a trinket merchant who had discovered diamonds in a zircon-studded cereal bowl. He wound around his bed, party-style, and forebent to accept a cigarette I offered—a generic non-filter of all things, one of his own. It was a type of happiness that I'd seen in the eyes of many inmates, a searchlight blast at the end of so many years, all of them carpeted in darkness and stagnation.

I smiled and nodded my head, snapping a finger to his electricity and rhythm. Time would go quickly for him until the next letter; then it would begin dissipating in a clogging haze of questions and procedures. Jovine couldn't get him out and he knew it, much less make Lotus rich. If he endlessly attacked statutes on prison regulations, *maybe* the D.O.C. spokesman would apologize for the Sinequan. But nothing else would really happen, so why bother with a guy who could get food stamps on his own? We were the pursuers in this case, but Jovine could at least come across and offer a straight hand. What did he have to lose?

Instead he gave Lotus an underdose—that faint grain that distorts recognition and leaves you flat with an odd sensation. An ill feeling would materialize, a visceral mambo like a type of blueballs: this, for an inmate who would one day be released, jerking like farm machinery down public streets. Jovine knew this, yet he short-armed, or underdosed, Lotus with a meringue-type of rejection swill.

I thought of Sandi for a moment, and how she would have to fend for herself a while longer. She may never have a front room of sparkling knickknacks and oddball acquaintances, who would tell stories and buy soda, passing the day in fine form. I could almost feel something for her, because she was the one who was hot at the start, mainly for her brother's freedom. There was nothing for her now but analogous fetal regression.

I walked back to my cot and opened my locker, looking at the skydiver who smoked a joint. I thought of a number of ways I could have lied to Lotus, but none of them really made sense. I made a fist with my head and cursed Jovine, along with the free-booking parameters of law.

How would you like to be mounted by your double? I asked Jovine for starters.

My chest started pounding and I felt lousy. I had a headache, and my body was like extended brainweight. The clock began to go slow and there were no distractions; it was the old long road that never quit at the horizon. But as long as those hands didn't change direction, Lotus and me stood a chance.

I laid out on my cot and felt the blood snap through my head. Then I closed my eyes and waited for sleep as the clouds began robbing the noonday sun.

Steve Fisher

a laggard in blood-red love

Candles burn in my room tonight.
Clothes lay scattered over the rug on the floor.
The ashtray is filled with the long afternoon, and the
radio, bleeding, alternates Bach against a field of static snow.
We allow it to play quietly, like my hand in your hand,
and your hand in my hand, until the number six bus rolls north
past my window, and the music stands clear like eight sharpened rods.

Before us, no doubts. I roll to you, inhaling the perfume on your
neck, examining your hair as if watching a creosote harvest dyed
orange and set afire. Root-wild. Illuminant. Locomotive.
But I also notice darkness above the curtain rims and think:
the loss of sunlight, at any moment, helps to prepare me for death.
And quite possibly, my love, the same holds true for you.

But now we have ventured into the territory of each other.
Your fingers trace an abstract scripture upon my chest, and
my skin opens up like a series of vertical partitions.
I feel the sensations rise and become atmosphere, become you.
I think: everyone else is at the opposite end of the magnet.
Yet how long will the stars permit us to go on,

and let the candles burn in solace to our phantom senses?

One kiss, sugar doll. I'm merely a laggard in blood-red love, but
my motives are clean, and parallel the torque of this opening-up,
and dividing, of the master cell occurring in you and in me:
the mosaics, interritorial, where I discovered you
alive in a substructure of pigment, tissue, and bone.

Kiss me. Jump me, French me, kill me, and let's begin once more:
O mercy sweet Jesus Lord of Our Avenues, O mercy sweet sweat.

as Bach surely intended.

Rock Salt & Glissandos

And now the room is again tropical with the echo of our heat.
Your hair, your head on my shoulder, as Bach continues forth.
My eyes open, close, as I disregard how we've arrived at
this steady and tranquil level of ju-ju: just two animals drinking
from the same canvas, sharing jug water from a cheap purple cup,
while our skeletons lie smooth, ring chromatically,
polishing this thing that wants to advance and shine through us:
words emerging viola, as if placed inside two glass skulls.

I light a cigarette and stare at the bomb-bright ash that holds
your face calm, and radiant, in the Burgundy-dark nightfall.
Our presence binds us: two lovers exchanging secrets, yet
with no one, until the other, found to be real at the center

within the runes and knoblock of this cracked concrete city.

But the candles are fading to wick-bristle scrubs, and the
radio—chickenshit—is tricked-out with batter-dipped vocal
Sunday morning harmonies. I note, in the marginal light, one
blue nylon dangling from the bureau as I switch the radio off,
advising myself:

I have been held within my lover's arms, and tasted the starlight
on the back of her neck. I am pure in grace as we speak true heart

and far from the streets where I've
lived on my own hard blood at
war with a microbe of blue and red sirens
unintelligible.

Yeh.

Baby Cherry: I wanna put a straw in you and drink.
I wanna be your man until I'm a jar of powdered minerals.
And as we lay between the blankets to close down shop I begin
to feel us, mojo, communing above the rotation of our earth
and my small, rented room:

Steve Fisher

—breathing the signal,

—dividing the eye,

—still as a pineapple.

controlled populations

Unfamiliar with my location,
I learn quickly, of necessity, and make
the three mile walk from Northeast L.A.
deep into Eagle Rock territory.
I'm entirely strung-out.
My watch reads 8:50 a.m. when I alight
on an RTD bench, yet already the boulevard
appears oaken, as if the sun's been filtered
through a stack of darkened hot cakes.
Sick, jonesing, the haze comes up brighter
than the blood in my arteries, but the external
is incapable of reaching far enough to clear me.
I have ten minutes to wait. To listen to the
automobiles, to dread any footsteps, to cough.
Until Stanley arrives at nine sharp, with six
magic keys that will unlock his Rexall pharmacy.
My scripts are so large he has no use
for the pill tray. He simply lines numerous
One-hundred-count bottles before me, as I reach
for a spring water, and pass him my VISA.
I remain outwardly collected, but
start sweating in twenty-five octaves:
my DEA file is thicker than a chateaubriand, and
even my fingertips, while signing the tab, expand
in oily palpitations against his Pilot razor point.
As I exit, my balls must smell like a stag deer in heat.
So I utilize the Taco Bell restroom next door.
Though it requires effort and a bit of time, I
begin to feel as if I'm injesting halogen lamps
in tablet form. And sucking three or four Valium chasers as
I emerge, while also lighting a cigarette, I'm confronted
by a Rasta at the RTD bench:

"You smokin?"
"Yea."

Steve Fisher

"I be badly hurtin, mon. I get-a one offa you?"
"Sure."
(inhaling) "I'll remember your people."
"Generously, I hope."
"The Spirit, mon, the Spirit always be generous."

The smoke he expels unravels like a trouser leg, and I
notice his teeth discolored police-tape yellow.
He trails a rusted blue wagon one-handed along the pavement.
A belt looped over a flap shrouds his Rasta hip-hop.
I've got three miles to retrace and only two feet, along
with undeniable concerns and other impingements.
The Spirit, *paisano,* certainly is generous:
we're all controlled people when we suffer.

Rock Salt & Glissandos

one for an over-worked mantor

Having always been an insomniac,
and trying the various methods
   to conquer
this over the years—such
as chronologically naming the 20
streets running through my neighborhood
   north to south
   —geographically
minded, isn't sleep hanging in the hollows
   down there, down south?—,
and finding it too didn't
   rub the nut for me,
it was on to the next inquiry.

So I pulled the old B&W TV
into the bedroom, resorting it
   on the nightstand with
the notion it would be so dull I couldn't
help but drift into the deep. Weird
   dreams, maybe, but
at 0900 I could care less.

Of course, it didn't work.
But I think it was during
   Donahue
I heard a vacuum cleaner commercial I learned
something from, their hook being:

   THE POWER OF AN UPRIGHT
   IN THE PALM OF YOUR HAND.

Marvelous, I laughed learning:
   all I need
is a phony diploma, could
hitch to NYC & get a

31

Steve Fisher

  legit job
for the television wives –

writing dirty copy at a yearly 80K

Rock Salt & Glissandos

soap line

The prison's property room had a back door that opened to a small, wooden sally port. It was bordered by the yard office and the commissary windows. The barbershop was back there, if you walked through that rear corridor of the yard office, but the commissary windows — one for each yard — sat along the traffic ramp that everyone had to use.

The barbershop was run by the blacks, since the whites wouldn't circulate that close to the staff. And because they ran it like a club privilege, some very elite strutting took place. They converged — the Muslims, the blacks — seldom mixing with the others on that passage ramp.

But the commissary windows were simply *grated* to a shack-like bungalow that had trailer siding tacked down, all of it painted a very artificial, shadow-sucking yellow. It looked like a margarine stick, with exhaust pipes stemming up. And the color-wash blonde who operated this store seemed always to exalt herself, promenading behind the window grates like a manufactured goddess on a pull string.

Fortunately, for the population, two inmate employees did the real work of getting the store items out: you had five hours, one day a week, to buy your shit through the window. On a revolving schedule that sent upwards of two hudred inmates at a crack into line. Of the other eight hundred that lived on these yards, a majority — always — swarmed around the line and waited with their friends.

But now it was an alternate Friday. Clifford stood below the steps of the passage ramp, waiting with the others in the soap line. He was in front of the property room, where another line waited to pick up their packages. His line ran up the steps, then horseshoed to the left, across from the two commissary windows. And there, in the sallyport, at the back of the property room, a guard checked off your number and issued a lunch sack with a small grip of laundry soap. Like everyone else, Clifford had T-shirts, socks, and a few other things, to run through the washer in his dorm. All dirty, overdue.

But four lines, dead in the middle of a frozen afternoon. Clifford put his hands in his jacket pockets and leaned on one foot but felt he was communing—overall—with nothing greater than a steel post. He looked to the side of the commissary trailer, to the rows and rows of raw ribbon wire. It was coiled there in a corner, behind a three-story, chain-link fence. They were simply building more walls with it. They were building *in* from the perimeter, to the center of the yard. Two inmates from electric shop sat with it, out behind that fence, on a fork lift they used to cart the stuff around.

Christ.

It was shit. Nothing but shit. Of all the shit that Clifford had seen in his life, the Department of Corrections, unquestionably, was the ranking Anal Mother of them all.

Yet he relaxed, as the line took a step forward, and a resident walked by with his soap bag. It only meant moving a few inches, though everyone looked back—scouting—to see if there was a play to be made from behind. But instead of a joint being passed, the line simply responded to itself.

"Soap issue's getting damn small."

"Not surprising, since they're taking all of our clothes away."

A sweet commissary smell rippled the air where Clifford stood, and he imagined—momentarily—that his tongue was actually a sugar wafer.

"*No*, Mr. Darvette," came the voice of the color-wash, from the commissary window. "You're *still* on restriction."

Her voice had high, whirring overtones in it, as if she were speaking through an electric drill.

"But you *know* that was lifted last week," said Darvette. "I want some store, *now!*"

"Sor-ry," she said. "You'll have to take that up with Major Halt. *Next!*"

"If you was a man, they'd *kill* you at the bar," Darvette was yelling as he walked off.

But the deal was this: She and Major Halt worked as a team. He arbitrarily regulated who could go to the store, mainly, it seemed, to create tension on the yard. The color-wash then perpetuated it, through one-on-one confrontation. Like a setup. But they always got their rocks, especially when someone could be sent to the hole as a direct result of their scheming.

Clifford looked around. The property room literally sagged in the center. And the same guy he noticed ten minutes ago was still up at the window. What was going on here? At least three hundred people were kicking around.

But the soap line moved up a few feet, somehow in motion. Clifford was almost to the steps when a heavily tattooed youngster, who'd been hustling the store line, came up to someone who was standing in the soap line. The youngster's arms looked like ax handles, in fact, done over with pine-green stampings. He told the person behind Clifford that he wanted a haircut.

Rock Salt & Glissandos

"Cost you a pack of Generics for a haircut," he was informed. Clifford recognized the voice of a white barber.

"So if I give you a pack of Camels, can I get a trim on account?" asked the youngster.

"You must be freshly jacked-off to say something like that," laughed the barber, then the whole rear ribbon of the soap line laughed too. Clifford laughed as well, but the deal was soon straightened out.

A jailhouse lawyer walked by with a client, though Clifford didn't bother looking them over. Both of them had their heads bowed.

"*State* law put you here," the lawyer was saying. "You gotta think *federal* federal federal federal."

They passed along, seemingly determined, chins tucked into their necks.

Then a couple of young Mexicans tried cutting into the store line. They yelled for a minute, insisting their homeboy had been marking their place. But an older Mexican booted them out, tired of all the juvenile bullshit.

Someone up front started saying, "Yeah, J. B. only come down with a year, but he took it all the way. He punched that guard sitting up there, an' they give 'im the twenty-five flat."

Clifford looked up to see an old guard, half asleep, sitting in the only chair on the ramp. He wondered, hazily, what kind of a pension a guard was entitled to for taking a single punch.

"That's the problem with these short-timers," he heard someone else say. "They don't know enough to kill these fuckers. You end up doing the same amount of time."

"I hear from the walls," the other guy said, "that that's what he's working on now."

The line moved forward again, and Clifford was on one of the steps. A gust of wind blew upon him, like something out of a withdrawal sweat.

"Sor-ry, Mr. Applegate, today just isn't your shopping day," he heard the color-wash say.

Clifford saw Applegate simply rage, while the color-wash smirked as if she were flattered. It was an ugly confrontation. Pit rage. She acted like a bullying tomboy, cursing in a play lot.

"Listen," Applegate told her, "you were the one who said I could shop here today. You told me on Tuesday. Now it's Friday. And now I need to get my stuff."

"No, no, Mr. Applegate, I told you to CHECK FIRST WITH MAJOR HALT about shopping here today."

"*Bull*shit!" said Applegate.

"That's what I told you," she said, crossing her arms against her rounded pot belly.

"Then you can just jam your fucking store up your ass," he told her. "I'll find your fucking kids!"

"OUT OF THE LINE!" some of the punks began yelling. This, too, appeared to make her feel good.

"Report to the yard office immediately!" she told him. She was ready to have him rolled up—sent to the hole—for cussing out the staff. Or, in truth, for assuming *her* attitude of indifference. But Applegate walked off in the other direction.

What crap, Clifford was thinking. She burrows into this system like a fucking sewer scabie.

"You *won't* get away with this!" she yelled at Applegate through the grate. Then, to the faces looking in, and with a smile as she tilted her head to the counter, "He may not know it, but I'm a true women's libber."

"WOMEN'S LIB NOWADAYS IS THE POLICEMAN'S AUXILIARY!" someone shouted back in.

"This state soap just rips up my laundry," an old convict said as he passed Clifford with his sack. He looked totally unmoved by the ramp, by the color-wash.

Clifford took a few steps up, landing on top of the passageway. He could look right into her window. And there, from the soap line, he saw the remedial dynamics to which she affiliated her life: she was shitting with pressed cheeks, and enjoying it. Which, in turn, sired malice on the yard. He wondered if the state's judges were also aware of this interaction.

Clifford listened to the pop of feet, as a Muslim worked his way to the barbershop. The Muslim's shoulder and pinky finger were in sync as he walked, his heels hitting the wood over thudding echoes. But the entire ramp was studded with crashings, as inmates kicked by on the boards. The vibrations bled through Clifford's muscles. Spired his bones. And a cadence was there, to which he felt a tonality. This, he thought, is how good music comes about: by listening to the streets, to the soap lines. It bolstered his energy as he waited.

The snap of another's observation broke through, as the line moved forward once again.

"You *become* 'dangerous' when you can outsmart the cops. They don't like getting burned, see, so they'll claim you're dangerous when you're able to pull jobs cleanly. But it's only a *term* that they broadcast. Whether they catch you or not, they're really just soliciting funds."

"Man, they're always trying to scare people," the other one said.

"ROSCOE!" hollered an unseen inmate, over in the cove of the sallyport. "YOUR CASE WOULD BE LIKE ASKING THE GOVERNOR FOR A PARDON AFTER RAPING HIS GRANDDAUGHTER!"

Clifford was directly across from the commissary window, about an armspan from where she leaned on her counter. It wasn't as if he'd never looked at her before, because he'd seen plenty of her since arriving on the yard. It was, however, just this thing of her face: she had eyelids like tissue paper, painted a light pink, shaping her skull like the head of a doll. Into something unnatural, stillborn and plastic. Into something that said she was asphalt and blank.

Rock Salt & Glissandos

He turned his head up and examined, for a moment, the roof of the yard office. Three electrical wires, black and lucent, traced against the greenish, winter clouds like an image in crayon from a child's hand. And he realized that, for as long as he'd been in this camp, he'd never seen a bird. Or an insect. Not even so much as an ant. Only big blue flies that ate wood and flesh, and buzzed around like generators during the long, hot months.

Clifford sawed his foot against the boards as faces slashed by, his hands sweating just a touch. The soap line had stalled, and the voices grew loud, giving him the odd sensation of being mobbed in a boxcar. Then the wind drove through, like a dust storm ejected by plunger from a dam. Fossils cycloned in the earth and separated — bits of ancient Indian lore — blowing up his legs, through his jacket — also into his mouth and eyes — making him feel as if a tightening had occurred, and he was trapped in a dry-heaving lung.

Exactly like that. Exactly like that. Always this further strain of constriction. He'd seen it drive some inmates mad, with the sickness of self-consciousness. And almost anything, at that point, could happen.

"HIT IT!" stated a voice to his right.

The fork lift roared in acceleration, a spring of razor wire lifting on its tongue. The exhaust shot out like an explosion. A guard was standing by an open section of the fence, supervising by presence, as the two inmates worked to guide the thing off. To a worn-down plot that once housed the tool shack, but now just looked like a ditch that'd been leveled. The reason for this construction was Major Halt, who also delighted in feelings of power and restriction. It served no other purpose than his sadism.

Absolutely.

But this was the time. Clifford had no way at all to foresee it. That statement came down through the soap line:

"They're fixing to get her."

It happened quickly, in the camouflage of traffic. With the howl of the fork lift, and off-center whistling. As five convicts semi-circled in front of the ramp guard, blocking his view of the color-wash. Of the window.

The color-wash stood there, marking on a file, doodling. Her face was down but the line was ready, as an inmate came up to the window with a glass. It was full of piss. Hot, foamy urine. It splashed on her cheeks, her hair, running down her chest through her unbuttoned collar. The upper portion of her uniform, normally tan, darkened like a sponge that had soaked up red wine. Her eyelid pink, and the rest of her powder, just mixed like a smear on light-colored cork.

The ramp fell silent, as everyone waited for her reaction.

The first thing she did was scream. She may not have known what just hit her, but she knew enough to realize that she *was* being attacked. The next thing she did was slam the grate closed. It was a huge steel plate that swung on a hinge, from inside of the window. There was a *slap* as the pieces connected. But the plate bounced away, forcing her lids open as she searched around—claw-like—with her fingers to lock it. The urine on her lashes burned her eyes.

The guard jumped up. Well, what could a guard do? He was just a trail version of the Old West, punched-out, and the yard had been pushed to an edge short of murder. He stuck his arms out, making motions, flappings, oil pouring from his face.

But the lines had already started to dissolve. There was shouting—loose congregating—but mostly the sound of the store being kicked. Kicked. Smashed. Punched. Body slammed. Among low, angry voices, sustaining this *cry*.

Then the blacks came running from the barbershop, ready to jump in on whatever was happening. But instead of a looting, the guards poured forth from that same door to the yard office. Fast. With riot sticks. Because someone had radioed, probably from the window of the property room.

Just the rampant commotion of bodies.

Only now boiling down.

But slowly, sluggishly.

Over the loudspeaker came a warning: "BACK TO YOUR CELLS AND NO ONE WILL BE HURT! THE YARD IS CLOSED! THE YARD IS CLOSED!"

Of course, it was bullshit. People had already been hurt. They'd been thrown against the side of the store. And maybe the color-wash would suddenly go blind with the MDS. It was a fear crossing her mind as she toweled down with Ajax.

But, in essence, the point had been made: give some respect to the residents, who also were the workers, and were forced to shop at a store they had no say in—except through extremes. It would seem like only a simple understanding, yet it was beyond the games that were played by authority.

"CLEAR THE YARD!!! CLEAR THE YARD!!! THE YARD IS CLOSED!!! THE YARD IS CLOSED!!!"

The yard barker—like a voice, male, from out of a sewer line—repeatedly blasted the camp. On and on and on . . .

But Clifford had cleared out, quickly, with the rest of them. The panic across the ramp was now a few strays, inmates who'd been crushed into the side of the store. Now it was mainly a topic. Now they had given warning. The dorms filled up and people went through them, talking, commenting, waiting for an emergency head count. Clifford sat on his bed and rolled up a smoke. He was thinking, still, of something else: the problem of his laundry.

But what a fucking joke, he was beginning to realize.

They had the count cleared in less than an hour. The cops did, that is. The yard reopened, though the store remained closed. But it wasn't as if they had to protect against a race riot. All they had was an incident, an *incident* to keep from going any further. And that could be handled, at the moment, because the color-wash, now, was out of the car. With the yard open again, Clifford locked up his cell. He stuffed an old skin magazine down the front of his jacket.

Rock Salt & Glissandos

And walked over to Roy's.

Roy ran a store, a canteen, from out of his house. Zum-zum's, wham-wham's, detergent, hopefully. Clifford just pulled out the magazine. He stood with Roy, looking at the pictures. Said what he needed was a box of soap.

Roy opened his locker. Clifford had a choice between Dutch Boy and Generic. The Dutch Boy was a tall large box, possibly good for two-dozen washes. He dropped the mag down, onto Roy's bunk. Or into his office, depending how you look at it. He was getting tired of those bitches, anyhow.

He went back to his cell. Pulled out his laundry. What the state issued, however, he easily held in one hand. But really, though, no matter. Long as he didn't have to crawl into the same orange jump suit, like he had to do in the old days. It was just a pain in the ass, to keep doing laundry.

Clifford walked to the laundry port, a space off the day room, lugging the clothes on his shoulder in a fishnet sack. He noticed the day room was crowded with sullen, low faces. He cut to the machines.

He sat his fishnet on the dryer, adjusted the washer button, and opened the lid. It was filled with trash, with blue water. And it stank like the air in a porter's closet. He was pissed, though not surprised, because the physical reality always pushed in. *Repeatedly* pushed in. From any side that was there: the Major, the color-wash, lock downs, soap lines. On routine chores that most people take for granted. But, to Clifford, it was all like staring at an octagon of reflectors: different angles, different metrics, but always the same slice of shit.

He walked off. Out, into the day room. It smelled of death scented with stale shirts and old sweat, balanced upon glaring youth. But nobody was paying him any attention. At all. He went back down the run, again got his jacket, and went over to Roy's pod with his fishnet.

Their washer was clean.

Clifford faked out a guard, a fish. The guard was stationed, there in Roy's dayroom, to keep non-assigned residents from cruising around. The guard scooted off, nose open to the chickenshit rules, and Clifford was able to run his clothes. As he loaded the machine, dumping his soap in, he began thinking how the wars on the yard affected everyone: cops, staff, flunkies, the inmates. And, on top of the wars, how all in the population had their own battles, personal battles, including the prick who had jammed the washer. Clifford's, at the moment, was simply getting his laundry done. But he was lucky not to be standing in the usual line of twenty.

He found a seat in Roy's day room and sat down. Hardly self-conscious, but prepared if the cop happened by. He rolled up a cigarette and lit it, inhaling, staring at the walls as the laundry machine shuddered.

Fumed.

Burned.

What a joke.

His expression was homeboy jazz.

Steve Fisher

a quick ugly dream between luxury hards

I awoke
with a bloodstalk
in the coarse pepper jail light
as the morning pumped out
with darkness & hollows.
   then muscled to sleep
     as a taste punctured my skull,
dreaming her face across a dog track—

   just a stray female gauze,
a flare of teeth & pouches
   through the echoing pillars:
her snack-counter clock eves
   & whisk broom brows
     daubed to an odd oval gust
   & cold grandstand steel,
the rafters peopled with burnt paper matches—

   they were like fish
attracted to structure
   & the creases you'll find in the fold of a raincoat,
   but thankfully, just one of her—

there was a dense circulation of content
   & dirt weed
     & dust hounds
& fat as it bubbled on a grill.
   far off,
like fingernails seen on your outstretched arm . . .

& mother mary was an old plump matron,
   a jailer in britches
     & boots
patrolling an unwashed corridor

Rock Salt & Glissandos

god, the dream was an eggbeater . . .

But then a thin molecular shift
   & again I awoke

   sweating a sausage-like film

       a work horn going through me

my head flubbing like a rubber wedge —

   but
   outside my cell
   the sky matted with antelope heads
   & daybreak
   corn lace

& it was time to take the law into my own hands again.

Steve Fisher

skull monkeys

> Get my ether!
> —Duke Ellington

I'm at a mailbox I seldom use.
A curb side or walk-up combination.
The curb side is overflowing, so I
park, exit, move toward the walk-up
with a singular letter, applying for
credit I know will be denied.
But just as I hit the pavement, the
unfortunate: a man and a woman, young
entry-level MBAs, appear as a growth
(near as I can fathom) at the
mouth of the mailbox,
trays of corporate swill
outstretched in their arms.
Their very *punctual* arms.
Tremors have overtaken me in
such situations before,
as if the *Red River* stampede scene
jumped my needle-thin nervous system,
hoof by two-ton hoof,
while prone and immobilized,
waiting.
God, lady. Fuck, man. DO IT!
I light a cigarette and notice
how stern and demanding
gravity is
while you're standing on concrete.
And he says, "Let me get this for you,"
pulling the handle back, all those
incorporated parcels dropping delicately,
leaf by leaf, from her hands
into the chute.

Rock Salt & Glissandos

I feel cheated.
They saw me.

Yet eventually her trays are finished,
and now — time in rags — it's his move.
Quite politely, she looks at him
and speaks: "I'll pull it open, if
you think you can get it in."
I appraise their faces upon this remark,
but their expressions stand still, untouched.
Shit, I wonder.
Despite the fact they're 3000
barrooms behind me, I fail
to understand why neither of them
have reacted.

Skull monkeys. Figurine curriculums.
This is what streams thru my head.
Perhaps it's these overcrowded
sump-water institutions that youth
throttle wall-eyed from today.
Perhaps *The Firm* acquired them
for Burger King wages.
I stomp my *frajo* as his
last pack of mail is deposited,
and finally, stepping forward, see
the walk-up is now jammed. I get back
in my short, ignite her, and decide to
leave the envelope in my home box
for our mailman.

It's cut-rate MBAs like these,
I'm thinking, who've spoiled my credit rating.
And now, the mailbox. For everyone.
Clearly, a perfectly sculpted duplication
of pricks.

Merging on the Ventura Freeway,

Steve Fisher

I plot to do them in.
I'll throw a party. I'll hire a Jeeves
instructed to spill it all in their
laps, not apologize,
nor bring a napkin
or a refill. Only the fetters.
Then onward, to the De Sade.

And if I can't locate those
two in particular, L.A.
is supple with replications:

not much difference between

   Joe the Jailer

across the room from

   Jerry the Jailer:

the play list is identical,
the play list is endless.

That, for starters.

basic pharmacy

Nulls me
from a jammed rally plaza
of

   Pro-lifers

   Politicians, anti-
   lifers

   Leafleteers

   Pamphleteers

   Circulators,

   Muck-cause
activists, contributor's box outstretched —

   My
   basic pharmacy

mellows me
on the same bench
or bed
or, say,

collaborating lumber

of indigestion or insomnia
which stated the same
intolerance to begin with.

   Basic administration

won't leave a crowded

Steve Fisher

head
stumped in raddling,

   simplified,

head-jammed stomping masses

until

   active,

completely necessary thermal

   bloodstream warmth

   & settling

settles in.

variations on the robe

Tony came down with the other fish one afternoon, a bit chubby with jail fat, but otherwise looking like a typical side street youngster: crystal meth, filtered cigarettes, smart hands under the hood of a Chevy. His pale, bright skin set his large eyes glowing in the sun, but he appeared somewhat yoked about having to do iron time: just distanced by youth, from the constant atmosphere of domain in a prison. It looked like he'd run with the perpetuated street trends, unaware of who ultimately controlled them, still disbelieving after months and months of judicial robes: even now, as he waited outside the yard office with the eight others in his train, wearing his first state-issue and lugging the olive green duffel bag. He was young, impressionable, fresh. Obviously so. He was here on his first number.

In fact, the judge had given Tony seven years for his part-time work in a Phoenix chop shop: He'd made two-hundred dollars every Saturday afternoon, customizing interiors on a variety of stolen cars. In a garage somewhere around his old neighborhood. It was one of the few things he knew how to do, and about the only skill he had picked up in high school. And besides selling small amounts of crystal, infrequently, to his friends, it was also the only way he had of making money. He was just standing in the dirt, about twenty feet from the fence which separated the yard office from the yard proper, sucking on his cheeks. The guards were inside, ritualizing the procedure of simple housing assignments. He didn't know anyone on the yard.

"Hey, you *pussy*-packin' motherfucker! I'm talking to *you*, punk!"

A group of convicts had lined up at the fence. They were looking over the arrivals, welcoming them with hatred, stares, low prospects. It was something institutional, learned by the rote of abnegation. It was like a sort of self-induced retching.

Tony felt the air around him scale down to a chokehold. He gripped tighter on the handle of the duffel bag, an icy smoke dampening his armpits. But his major conflict was the reaction to look: to spin his head around from the glare of the yard office, and look at the faces wandering the fence. Instead he moved in a half-motion and froze. But he noticed someone else had turned completely around, almost as if summoned by the calls. Tony just waited there in an awkward stance, feeling his heart race, feeling encumbered.

"You little shit-faced asshole," the fence said to the guy who had turned around. "You'll be coming out of that gate in a minute, won't you?"

"*Won't* you, you little fucking punk!"

It was thrown out to the arrival like a contrary revelation. Tony still didn't know what to do, but knew enough not to feed into the fence or to play on the side of the guy who had turned around. The turn around was trapped: by the inmates who darkened the fence up ahead, and by the guards, behind him, who lounged in the yard office. Tony was straight off the D.O.C. bus. But even though there were eight others with him, Tony felt he may have telegraphed an emotion: a feeling, some flesh, an instinct that occurred through personal habit. The sensation came through that he'd also been busted—or caught with his youthful responses—and he would now have to deal his way out as if he had, in fact, actually spun around and faced the onlookers at the fence. But he couldn't be sure. It could go either way. A rock skipped by in the dirt near the turnaround, and Tony decided to hold his position. It was as if he'd barricaded himself in a silk lining from a stampede, but this was the spot he was forced into now. Then he slowly became aware of a hinge squeaking in a far-off, unknown direction within the complex. It sounded like the tune of a large dying bird—a five-note zigzag pattern that ended with a bugle call—and went directly to his head like it was being massaged through his skull. He listened intensely, staring at a doorknob on the yard office, his peripheral vision closing with blackness. The catcalls and yelling continued, like arrows fired at stranded prey on a shoreline.

"Think you been *bad*, huh punk?"

"Motherfucker looks about *lame*."

"They *all* be lookin' like lame-ass bitches!"

"And you right here at the gate, motherfucker . . ."

That strange, five-note zigzag played in Tony's head. He lost track on which side of him it originated, the inside or the out. His knees tightened around an impulse to somehow break away: seven years at half-time, ninteen years old. The darkness took everything, blackened Tony's surroundings, until he looked as if he was standing there in a coma. The turnaround only pulled his face inward with terror at the shouting . . .

Out on the yard it was hot. The winter air that had been around for ages, it seemed, blew off one night and the sun came through. It had baked the camp to a hard desert crust. This heat made you feel like you were in the lungs of

Rock Salt & Glissandos

a fever patient, even when accustomed to it. But since this was only the first of the season—late March south of Tucson, not more than a parade banner from the Mexican border—the inmates on the yard moved slow, moved sluggishly, as they went about their institutional routines: the rock rakers coughed, the maintenance workers only carried one tool, the land porters pretended to find trash in the shade. And the scoring in the softball game mostly resulted from infield errors. It was over ninety degrees out, even in those thin spottings of shade, but most of the population had come out to mill around and to circulate. The dirt on the yard had been scraped down to the plow.

I was leaning against this useless fence near the tool shack with someone I didn't know, called Razor. Tony and the other arrivals weren't far from us, just a handscope across the walkway to the right, which Razor kept pointing out to me while he tried getting a line on them: "I think *all* them's straight off the tuna boat, except maybe for that one on the end," he would say. I didn't really care who they were, since I hadn't recognized any of the faces. I was only there for the sun, to work my skin and to get away from the dorm. I only wanted to get some air.

But I squatted and looked over again, while the teams left the field and exchanged gloves for a new inning.

The nine of them had lined up in the dirt, and were waiting for the guard to come back with some instructions. They all faced the yard office, except for the turn around, in the direction of the single, rectangular window. It had been painted a dark, eggplant-like pigment about two-thirds of the way up. This way the guards could peek out, as they wished, but the arrivals couldn't look in and see what was happening. The guards figured it really didn't matter: this was the last American exit, a place where acknowledgment no longer was required. But most of the arrivals had worried, expectant looks on their faces, and the fence continued to demand recognition. The turn around, in particular, looked like he was counting on the guards to take care of matters for him.

But they didn't.

A young, sarcastic officer, thin as an oar, came out with a clipboard and began yelling names, numbers, dormitory assignments. He read them quickly and looked at no one. He just arched his voice in a cocky, authoritarian front, then quickly ducked back inside. Nothing more. Didn't even bother asking if anyone had questions. Tony was only told "4-E-10." So was the turn around. All of them walked slowly toward the gate, in silence, their eyes fixed out on the sprawl of the yard. It was like dropping sea horses into a tank full of piranhas. Tony's heart swelled up and beat red flashing punches.

"Lookit this here *boy* comm' along," said the fence.

"I think we got us a *prime* cut," said another, all of them looking at the turn around.

Tony sensed that he wasn't being picked out of the line by finger pointing,

49

but the static which jumped through his legs almost made him lurch into the inmate in front of him. They were going so fucking slow. Or they weren't going at all, it was hard for him to tell. But he *could* hear the *p-foot p-foot* of their heavy boots scraping along. It gave him some comfort, though really not much, but he was relieved he hadn't been booked from a moment ago when he'd nearly spun his head to the voices.

"Hey Lonnie, why don't you go *scout* this thang for me? I'll be wanting to stop in and pay him a visit."

"Alright, Eliot. Know it's your world."

As one of the convicts moved to follow the turn around, Tony knew that a judgment was being made. He didn't come close to understanding this in terms of the parliamentary yard, but he knew enough to realize that control *was* being placed on someone. He was just glad it wasn't him. The thing that mattered at this point, he thought, was to simply keep his bearings straight.

He moved across the yard with the duffel bag on his back and the zigzag out of his ear: it was a sound much too isolated for him to keep up with. He felt the eyes upon him as he crunched through the dirt, the gravel, on the walking track to his dorm—which was lettered in huge, block numerals on the outside, minimalizing some of his confusion—but he wasn't sure about the jeers, the whistling, that went on around him. He ignored it best as he could, feeling his face as the sun brought the salt to his skin. Maintain, he thought, I've just got to maintain. The turn around, again, was the one having real problems: stumbling along, close to a panic, and rapidly sucking down quick short breaths.

But the seven other arrivals had pulled different housing. Tony knew that the scout was behind them, behind him and the turn around, moving from the fence and watching. He felt awkward being one of the few inmates, among hundreds, who carried a duffel bag out there—a bit rubbery in the head, and marked by contrast—but the dorm came up sooner than expected and he plowed through, locating the E-wing.

He got lucky.

Tony found his bunk, and within five minutes had unloaded the crap in his duffel bag—just heavy state clothes which he threw into a small, metal locker. He noticed a card game going on a few houses down but he still didn't know what to do, just what would be expected, though the tension he felt suddenly shifted as the turn around screamed from out in the dayroom. About twenty people sprang from his wing and ran down the aisle, to look on, some peering from the glass that boxed off the guard's cage but most of them pushing through the door. Tony was among those who watched from the inside, looking through the glass and thick wire screen.

But nobody was even *on* the turn around. He had come through the entrance of the day room, overwhelmed by the consequences of spinning in the arrival line, to break from an inability to think he could resolve the matter in his favor. To simply stand up for himself, should he later be forced to do so. He was up against the cinder blocks, wedged to the telephone frame, his eyes loaded with fear and mistrust. His arms were raised chest high and he flapped them comically, like a puppet chopping wood in a department store window.

The inmates in the day room gathered round.

"Fucker's having an attack," someone shouted.

"No, he's freaking."

"Need *Thorizine!*" a high voice suggested.

"Don't crowd him. He might convulse and hurt you."

The open-lung screams that came from his terror were now hollow, thin, throaty grunts and moans. Tony put his palm on the cage window, intrigued and a bit frightened, watching the house cop run up the corridor. The cop had his radio in hand, but tried making sense of the situation before doing a thing. Ugh. Always a disadvantage, when crucial calls are handled by minds jobbed on authority. The red tape rolled through the cop's head and went nowhere—you only picked up on his impulse of crowd control—but two other C.O.s heard the yelling from outside. They came in, parting the crowd with spear-like arm gestures. The turn around only had a distant look in his eyes, like he'd been watching a horror show through the barrel of a microscope.

"This ten-fifteen properly managed?" one C.O. asked, everyone silent.

"I think we ought to get him out of here," said the house.

"Looks like he mighta been smoking that jimson weed them guys in horticulture bring back."

"I got a pair of cuffs," said the other C.O., snagging the turn around's wrist while his partner grabbed the kid in the arm pit. The turn around gasped as he was slowly led away, out through the door, into the view and summation of the entire yard. A sort of mucous was forming in the corners of his eyes.

"Where they taking him?" asked Tony.

"C.D.U.," an older con said in a heavy Southern accent. He began walking off.

"That around here?" Tony asked, following the others.

"Shit man, that's lockdown!" said a tall, muscular guy.

"Central Detention Unit," someone schooled him.

"That motherfucker just got off the bus with me," Tony informed them. "Look at the shit that goes on around here."

"Happens all the time, man. This is a really fucked-up joint."

Tony, now, was more interested in the contact he was making: he didn't want to end up like the turn around. He followed the Southern accent and the muscle back to their card game. The accent was Chester. The muscle was Chop-Chop. Tony latched onto them.

"What do you think they'll do with that guy in C.D.U.?" asked Tony, leaning into the cubicle wall.

They weren't exactly eager to talk with a fish, and let the question pass. Tony looked down and pursued them through their card game.

Steve Fisher

"You guys is playing poker, huh? Whadaya call this game?"

Chop-Chop deliberated on a card, then said, "Split-Ace thirty-one."

"Never heard of it," said Tony, "and I played *all* types of poker." He then asked, "What is it?"

Chester dropped the K of diamonds on an unconnected run of cards, stared down, answered "*Sheet!*" to Tony's question. Tony drew his head up and looked through the run.

"How long'er you in Alhambra?" asked Chop-Chop. He was still looking at the board.

Tony looked back at him, feeling good because he'd been asked something.

"Three months," he said. "And I was in the Phoenix jail for almost a year before that."

He waited. Somebody in one of the end cubes turned up a loud, pop-metal tune on the radio, but just as quickly turned it back down. The dorm was like dusk. Chop-Chop threw out a card, then looked up and studied Tony.

"It was fucked-up," Tony told Chop-Chop, looking into his eyes. Chop-Chop's face was narrow, a flatiron, beneath rust-colored hair. Tony was confidant about the description.

"Just wait 'till you been round here awhilst," said Chester. "This is where fucked-up breeds like a kennel."

"Yeah it is," said Tony, noticing Chester's missing lower teeth. He was stocky, a mid-age fellow with sandy-blonde hair, and his forehead was creased unlike anything Tony had seen before. Six of his front teeth were missing, and he had these two old fire plugs rotting in one corner of his mouth. But Tony only saw fat yellow teeth. He looked into Chester's eyes.

"Met your cellie yet?" asked Chop-Chop, a grin on his face.

"Fuck no," said Tony, laying his arms on the ledge and cracking an ankle. "What's wrong with him?"

"He's a shit-sick lame," Chop-Chop told him, laughing with Chester about something that was known. Tony looked at the two, wondering, biting the flesh of his cheeks with his molars.

"Ya don't want no *lames* cellin' down with you, do ya kid?" asked Chester.

Tony already knew how to handle that one. It was becoming obvious to him.

"Fuck a bunch of lames," he said, but his answer didn't matter. Another inmate walked out of the run and Chester leaned back, slapped down a card, yelled "Git that fucker to turn them *coo*-lers on in here!" Tony watched as the guy said something to the house cop, who then rolled on his chair to a corner of the cage. He flipped a switch with the key. The vents over Tony's head popped like enormous beer cans, squealed, and blew dusty air throughout the run.

But the swamp coolers weren't bothering him at all. In fact, the remark about his cellie didn't register much either, because now he was talking—communicating—*siding* with people, the same people who were going to be his neighbors. It either clicked *fast* in these situations, or it didn't happen at all: Tony knew that from the county lockup. But what he didn't know was that Chester ran a store, employing Chop-Chop as one of his collectors. And he couldn't have known what all of that meant, except it was hustle, and some of those moves he'd learned on the streets.

Yet he did feel that a sort of initial gray webbing had been lifted, and was gradually being replaced with something solid: solid in contrast to Alhambra, to the Phoenix jail, and certainly in contrast to the turn around. Chop-Chop offered a fresh pouch of tobacco: good deal, thought Tony, since for months he'd been twisting up snipes in Bible paper. He moved to Chester's bed and rolled a handful, loosening his shoulders, paying little attention to the card game in this dark, rectangular prison run. Just having worked through this blind spot was the important thing, he felt, the thing so much else would be resting on in tone. He bummed a lighter and fired up the rollie. He sucked the smoke down, alert, feeling as if he would fit in after all.

Out on the field, the ball game was almost over. The Repeat Offenders had something like a twenty-run lead over a new team, The Lay-Ins, but I wasn't much interested. I was stretched in the dirt, leaning against a fence near the perimeter. It felt good to be out there in the heat, to know the cops hadn't yet discovered how to regulate the sun. I gazed as a cloud went past in the shape of an angel fish. I looked long and hard though completely at ease, rather feeling I was in a vase, looking up at the petal on an imaginary flower. Then I dropped my eyes to the roof above a dorm, to the flags waving on the pole outside of the complex. A roll of clouds bunkered in the southwest, over the Mexican flea town of Agua Prieta, beyond the flagpole but not far from our camp. They looked dark, gummy. Tense, actually, and suspended as if in a slingshot. Like the 4:00 p.m. lock down count, they would soon be upon us.

I gathered up and started walking, on the track, just as the game was being called. I managed to get two laps in before the curfew horn sounded, circling on the partial lap back to my dorm. Dorm 4-E. Bed twenty-six. I got in and Tony was just down the run from me. I recognized what was happening by the way he hung out: the loud voice, the posture, the way he adjusted to play the residue which sifts through the restrictions. He was bargaining with Chop-Chop and Chester, working a deal to collect for the store. But too fast, too quick, he had no idea what he was getting involved with. Really no idea at all.

Then the clouds thundered in and it poured for a few days. I was forced to hang around, inside the house, and listen as Tony matured as a thug. Or *tried* to mature. "Damn right!" he would say, or "Fuck them lames!" It hardly mattered what the question was: a majority of the game involved the status of being obnoxious. And, of getting away with it. This is how it happens. A few days later, when the rain let up, a weary admixture of convicted Arizona residents finally hit the yard again, that sunshine, that heat. "I got an assignment for you, youngster," Chester yelled down the ramp. I only hoped for sporadic peace and quiet, for random elevations of silence in the dorm. Though nothing had been spoken of the turn around, Tony, now, was becoming a clown.

Inside the dorm it was still hot: four inmates were near punches over a cigarette lighter that was missing from a locker, an unvented bag of brew had just exploded in someone's house, and Jesse—in the head—was sitting on the crapper shooting junk with a binky: a cut-down syringe (minus plunger) that's been modified with a paper cap, then held on the rig with a rubberband. Bloody ragged and rough time. The coolers blew hard and Pine-Sol was mopped around, but the run still smelled like an animal pound that had been slickened with canned peaches.

I was busy with a mattress I'd just acquired. Tony's roommate, only in the cube a few days, had been run out of the pod by Tony when he found that the guy was a laxative freak: he had all sorts of pills and creamy shit that he drank, ritually, all day long, spending the rest of his time on the crapper. It almost appeared to be something sexual, but however it went it wasn't tolerated by anyone. It was, simply, gross. Tony threatened the geezer with a ball bat—to demonstrate his rising power—and the laxative freak was gone. Movement assigned him a new house. But the mattress was left, so I paid Brian a Coke to wash it down for me. Brian lived next door. He was, in his own way, a freak too: a sort of work-ethics freak. Yeah: there *were* some advantages to having these motherfuckers around.

But the observation lifting my head about the whole deal was this: the assemblage of power, in any given court, is fed primarily by skinning other people's action. You'd literally jump on someone's shit, *insist* it's your judgment, and have the physical means of backing your claim: the term on the street is Police. The term in the joint is Rule. And the attitudes of both were dictated by where the control, the profits could be made.

Yet the difference in prison was that you no longer had any doors guarding your life. They'd already been knocked down. Kicked open. And now you were among thousands, monitored at any given moment. Folks were grafted, by force, and clustered at this forefront, like suckerfish attaching to wet rocks in a drying ocean. Stark. Fragile. Skin-to-skin. But *Shakin' the Blues*. No chance (thank God) for a laxative freak, but I was noting the process of power. Of Tony's growing stature. And I was also tired of sleeping on a bed that felt like the slats in a cargo hold.

I had my usual mattress propped against the cube wall when Tony charged in. Brian was fitting the new one on my bunk, sliding it under: I didn't want contact with it, even through a sheet. Tony came along with a large paper bag, but overnight I noticed that he'd developed a slightly forward incline. And had worked his shoulders into a span, going for the look of The Posture. His caterpillar eyebrows blew under the coolers, but his hands turned outward and dangled like little rakes.

"Where's *Ches*ter!" he yelled down the run. Three days, and already he

Rock Salt & Glissandos

thought of the dorm as common rental property.

Chester didn't hear because he was wearing his headphones, lying in bed, and watching cartoons on the television. But Tony had swaggered halfway down the ramp.

"*Know* you's in here, Chester! Can't hide from me no *mo'*!"

This time, Chester heard.

"Bring it on *in* here, youngster," Chester yelled back. "We ain't doin' business olnst the goddamn streets."

Tony took it in and talked low, but still loud enough for anyone to hear him. He was sitting on Chester's bed when Chop-Chop strolled up to the cube's square mouth.

"Looky here at all this shit," said Tony, opening the bag for both of them to see. "I gots it offa that dude in building five. Just like you said, Chester."

Chester sat up, curling an index finger over the rim of the bag, his blonde hair pointed out like cane. But his eyes were straining to figure out what was in there. "Git the shit outta my face!" he finally told Tony, actually going somewhat cross-eyed.

Tony sat the bag down, allowing it a bit of light. I had top mattress set up, was working on my sheets, and noticed four who argued over the cigarette lighter had now moved off. Jesse, still, was in the head: nodding, perhaps. Drifting, zoned.

"We got us a bo-*nanza* sack," said Tony, getting in there with Chester and pulling out a bag of Twinkies. Chester reached and got the cigarettes from the bottom of the bag.

"Ju git all the Camels, youngster? What the fuck's these Pyramids?"

Chester was now sitting on his bed, with two packs of Pyramid's held off in one hand. With the other he slicked back his hair. He looked over at Chop-Chop as if to confer on a point:

"Now tell me I oughtenta wulp oln him like a red-headed stepchild?"

He turned to Tony:

"What *is* this shit, kid? Where's the other pack of Camels?"

Tony began pumping his right leg.

"Now, just you hold up a minute," he said. "I almost got throwed into the hole for those, cuz, uh, dude didn't wanna give 'em up. But I told him, 'Two packs of Pyramid's for the other Camel you owe, or we's fighting.' Dude didn't wanna, but he *seen* that look I get in my eyes. I'm tellin' yas, I was a fuckin' *cunt* hair from going to the hole."

Those tobacco-colored eyes sat far in Tony's skull, barreling out at Chester like copper slugs. He continued to pump his leg.

"Then ya done good," said Chester, arranging them on his bed. He reached and got the tally sheet from his locker — a list of dates, debts, customers, all done in code — while Tony dumped candy and sodas on the bed. Chop-Chop was borrowing a weight belt from someone — this tall, leather strap, worn to keep the spine from popping when you pump iron — draping it downward

Steve Fisher

from his shoulder to the waist. He was so fucking tall, but slump-shouldered and thin of neck, that looking at him from the back was like sighting a grounded rowboat. He then stood there, at the cube.

Chester held a pencil about an inch from his ledger, thinking. Tony, seemingly from instinct, was now telling him, "They's all two-fer-three collections, except for the Pyramids . . . let me get one of them peanut clusters, Ches."

Chester pushed a peanut cluster across the bed, his gray hairy backhand soft, like wool fluff.

"What elst ya need, kid?" he asked Tony. "I can't be erasing column B all afternoon."

Tony said, "Give me a couple of those donut sticks fer later, and a can of root beer for Chop-Chop. And another peanut cluster. Just ONE MO', Chester; *knows* you can do it!"

Chester mumbled something about his profits being eaten snarling, a bit, like a branch-whipped hiker. He told Tony as he slid the crap over, "Tonight, youngster. Remember you're collecting from Gomez. That motherfucking Mexican's been owing me for over a month now. *God*damn!" Chester stood up, looking at Chop-Chop, list in hand. "This motherfucker's so overdued you best shake him a little by the bed boards. He's up to five-fer-two right now, Chopper. Teach him a bit of respect."

Chop-Chop, who worked mainly for the sport anyway, knew all about the delinquent account. It was the way he killed time.

"You're covered," he told Chester. He then notched his chin up and said, "I'm hittin' the weight pile before they call chow. We'll bring the stuff by later." He tilted his eyes down to Tony's. "Comin'?"

Tony was sitting, still, on Chester's bed, making sounds with the peanut cluster cellophane. Crumpling it, balling it up. He stood, looking at Chester.

"I *was* gonna play bump n' touch with this here old man," Tony said, "but I guess we gots things to be doing right now — important things." He gave Chester a playful eye, elbowed into him. "I'll be back shortly for my workout snacks. Best lock 'em up, so's nobody steals them."

"*Buscala*," said Chester, as Tony walked off with Chop-Chop, but as he said it he spotted two cops coming through on patrol. He began stashing stuff, right and left, before they'd have a chance to look it over. He was, after all, running what they referred to as a "criminal enterprise." But Tony still didn't seem to know it. He told Chop-Chop, loud, as they passed the cops, "We'll be humping to-*night*, man. Eatin' and smokin' GOOD." Chop-Chop walked silently, squeezing the weight belt, ducking quickly out the door.

But Chester wasn't the only one scrambling as the two brown suits hit the run. Jesse, shades on, came from the head, and cut out of the dorm. *Fast.* A bottle of shampoo was poured on the fruit swab left from the metallic brew, and swirled with available feet. The ramp was noisy with the popping of locker doors, and I was scattering clothes over my bed. I had to. It was an offense to sleep with a double mattress — a mundane but *punishable* write-up—and I recognized those cops as Iron-Carpet-State radicals not capable of thinking beyond policy. And not willing to bend an inch. But deployed as yard officials, anyway, to simply sneak around and harass people. To moderate, police, and to *judge*. Luckily, my clothes were handy. The robes strolled by and didn't give me a second look. But I was certain they had noted what Tony just said, and would mark it on their form of "unusual inmate remarks." Tony only thought he was fully schooled. Yet he was as careless with his mouth as he was with sudden alliances. The cops just walked through, leisurely, like they were subordinate to a supreme purpose.

But nearly everyone, I was thinking, had been nibed so far down that they only existed in fleshy rubber saclets. Waiting for moves, plays, commodities, but functionless: Tony with the cartooning and speech of Mr. Attitude. The robes on the street corners, the corridors, sealing the exits with bugger holes. What could most people really do, when they weren't exerting the pressure of barriers? Again, I was starting to wonder.

Brian looked over at me as the cops checked the bathroom. His offer was to wash down the laxative freak's pillow, just for a few cigarettes. He held the pillow in his hand, outward a little, like he was bringing me the warden's head. I watched him stand there, adolescently. He claimed to have never, out on the streets, missed even one day of work.

"Pass," I told him, throwing the clothes into my rack. He looked dejected, so I fished out the Coke. But he should have felt grateful just putting in a half-day.

The cops left the bathroom. They headed out the door. Tony and Chop-Chop were at the weight pile by now, going through a routine. Chester laid on his bed like always, watching the cable, ready for trade when people came around. I left the dorm and stood near one of the perimeter fences. The sun was there, it caught me like a blowtorch, but those coolers were agitating allergies I'd never had. They blew in all manner of border town preparations, along with the usual dust and grime. But I never wanted Arizona for the air-conditioning. The coolers set me off. I sneezed pure rocket fuel for five minutes, then pushed away from the fence to walk along the track. And do no one's time but my own. If any odds-makers were around, I would've put high duckets on Tony becoming a slag personality. I just didn't know it would happen so soon.

Tony met Chop-Chop after count in the horseshoe pit. The agenda was Gomez. Their plan was to confront him in the chow hall and give warning: a warning that they'd be expecting a carton of smokes from him, or else there was gonna be trouble. Pain. Maybe a sticking. He'd have exactly one hour, and no partial payments. Two-for-five on four packs of Camels: a carton, including late fees. Tony wrote finger-tip messages on the palm of his hand, then ambled The Posture toward the chow hall.

Though the hall was packed, they got through the chow line quickly. I was there. With four hundred cons. And overhead lighting like a gray sheet of rain. But Chop-Chop knew plenty of folks, from around, so they were able to find seats in the rear. Tony, however, still didn't know who Gomez was. No matter: he looked around, until Chop-Chop pointed him out.

Tony raised himself, slowly, on the stool. A hub cracked in his lower spine. To his right he saw Gomez, small, a Mexican wearing the Cross around his neck. Tony couldn't see how short Gomez was: he only looked dark, rotund, stubby. But his hair was knickered to the scalp, and that did make him somewhat intimidating. It also looked like he would never smile again in his life.

Tony thought he could take him. That the macho expression was forced, like vanity practiced in front of a mirror. He stirred the gravy into his mashed potatoes with a spork, looking intensely at Gomez, his lips fattening, feeling heavy.

"He'll be one sorry *ese* without them smokes," Tony told Chop-Chop, the adrenaline pumping through his system. "Why'nt I go over and speak to him real casual-like?"

"Wait 'till it's cool," said Chop-Chop, nodding Tony to a guard stationed by the serving window. "When that cop goes into the kitchen, tell Gomez that *we* got something to tell him."

"Alright," said Tony, jerking his back.

Tony bit into the hot dog on his tray, chewing in the manner of a pike. There didn't seem to be any worth to it. He continued to stir his issue, watching the cop that stood near the ice machine. A door to the kitchen was off to the cop's left, along with an exit ramp used by the general population. The guard's assignment was to stand there as a force: make sure you took only one tray, one cup, and so on. But when he followed an inmate through the exit ramp, Tony dropped his arms and leaned back. His eyes darted over to Chop-Chop's.

"Now?" he asked.

"Cool," said Chop-Chop.

Tony lifted straight up from his seat, graciously, almost like a guest being honored at a banquet. Although he'd been collecting around the dorms, in a sense he was now going public: all these convicts, someone around any way he turned. It was like taking on more responsibility: a nineteen-year-old kid, first number, first beef. He kept Gomez in sight, weaving past the tables.

But there was one thing Tony hadn't taken into consideration: Gomez wasn't alone. He was with three other Mexicans, his homeboys, young, all of them knickered exactly alike. Tony thought he could give a shit. He bent to the shine on Gomez's bristles.

And gave him the word:

"You owes Chester a carton of Camels. Me and that tall over yonder's his representatives. You got ONE HOUR to up with them, or we's bustin' your head."

Tony straightened back up. But Gomez shook wildly and said, "*Get the fuck outta my face!"* Tony repeated it again: "One hour, starting NOW!"

This time others heard him, other Mexicans who were grouped in the area. A bunch of them turned, looking on. Tony was aware of them, but not of the cop who had returned to the ice machine. Now *he* was looking their way. Tony stared at Gomez for a moment, then started to walk off. But one of Gomez's buddies put his foot out. Tony went down on his ass.

It only took a moment for him to get up, but now everyone in the chow hall was looking his way—*their* way, actually, at the table where Gomez sat with his homeboys. And except for the giggling of a few young, scattered wetbacks, the chow hall was as quiet as an empty cage.

Tony got up.

Gomez got up.

About ten guards ran over.

But before any of them got to Tony or Gomez, Tony—sagging forward—punched Gomez in the eye: a real *amateur* fish move, in front of all those cops. As he started to get another one off, Gomez came up with a fist in Tony's jaw. Then one more, this on the side of his mouth. Any witness would swear self-defense.

Tony wobbled in place, dazed. He heard the screams, the sounds, the voices echo through the chow hall. Gomez, though, was stronger than he had anticipated. He hit Tony again in the same part of the jaw: a tooth popped from his mouth like a grapefruit section. But Tony, like a fool, with blood on his face, screamed, "You still owe Chester and I'm still collecting! Me an' Chop-Chop's gonna burn your ass good!" He just laid the thing out so everyone knew. He just gave up the whole operation.

The cops grabbed both of them. Quickly. Others stringed through the chow hall, in an attempt to prevent it from spreading. Two additional robes went searching for Chop-Chop, but he wasn't that difficult to find: he was towering over a sea of blue heads, erect as an electrical pylon. The guards pulled him slowly, carefully, over to the exit.

But the fight didn't matter anymore. At least to the convicts. What *they* couldn't stand, and what furthered the police economy, was the fact that Tony had snitched. In this case, actually, a dry-snitch: the non-intentional snitch of giving yourself up. But he had involved people other than himself. Lame, really lame. As the robes hustled to get him through the door a chant went up, LOUD and FAST, of *"KILL KILL KILL!—KILL KILL KILL!"* The cops worried that they might be ambushed, but the convicts knew better than to take him right there: the future was nothing but time.

They found Chester at home, TV on, cooking canned food in a hot pot and drinking a root beer. Relaxing. They told him he was needed in the yard office, and to lock up his cube. But even for an office call, there was something about this that didn't seem right. Chester, sensing gloom, protested that he didn't understand. That he would be pissed about having to leave his food.

None of it, however, impressed the robes. Chester shut down the appliances and locked his cell.

The chanting still came from the chow hall as they led him across the compound: "*KILL KILL KILL!—KILL KILL KILL!*" Chester couldn't quite make it out, yet he knew it had something to do with him: why else would they lead him away? As they came closer to the chow hall he spotted Tony and Chop-Chop. Handcuffed, being escorted from the hall by a small platoon of guards. He suddenly knew that his store had been busted. He watched them lock down the chowhall, but the chanting leaked out. Jesus, those fuckers were noisy! And *mad* beyond simple anger. He only guessed at what it could be: it really sounded, from the yard, where the three of them were being assembled, like two thousand ravens in the pit of a quarry, getting screwed in the ass by an army of vultures. The cops moved them cautiously, separately, to the yard office, leaving all of the details to the lieutenant on duty.

The charges for the three of them read as follows:
CONSPIRACY: 1 count
RACKETEERING: 1 count
EXTORTION: 1 count,
with an added charge of assault for Tony. The Sergeant mentioned additional violations, such as promoting a criminal enterprise, promoting prison contraband, and blackmail. The Lieutenant took off his specks and rubbed an eye while considering it. He paused like a break between innings.

"Go ahead and write it up," he told the Sergeant. "These motherfuckers can plead down in a court of law to forty years' hard time. Can you see the look on the judge's face when we bring them in?" The Lieutenant was motionless. He gazed at the wall before him, this glossy condition upon his face. He looked like he'd never been able to out-sleep a hang over. The Sergeant hit the *return* button on the Selectric III.

Chop-Chop and Chester were housed in the A-wing of C.D.U. The hole. They were given cells down the corridor from one another, and each had a roommate. Chop-Chop stretched out on the unsheeted rubber mattress, but Chester stood at the cage-front with his hands through the bars. He was pissed. Burned. He would say that, all along, he knew better than to ever trust a fish. Ever. But he couldn't quite figure why he had. He just stood there, the bars framing his mug in the gritty yellow light. He looked from the cell. The creases on his forehead rolled like postmark cancellations.

Tony was also taken to the hole, but placed in protective custody instead of the general population run. He'd be tortured to death as soon as the guards turned their backs, over with Chester and Chop-Chop, so they put him with the snitches in the P.C. unit. Tony knew it was the only choice he had. But he didn't know there were so many of them. Dozens. Like Chop-Chop and Chester, he was also given a cellmate.

The first thing the turn around told Tony was, "We're gonna have to look

Rock Salt & Glissandos

out for each other when we're transferred to the maximum-security ward. It's just down from a regular run. Those guys'll break in and do *horrible* things to us." He sat cross-leg on the lower bunk, trembling as he spoke, rubber headed from Thorazine and powdered with shadows. The cell was otherwise barren.

Tony just looked through the mesh covering of the P.C. bars, thinking of court and of all that *time*. He had no idea what he would do with it. Because not only did he suffer the walls, but rather an overhang which prevented him the inner-access of journey. It seemed to work like that on people favoring restriction, regardless of the colors, or variations on the robe. Just a system composed of lateral attacks: self-mutilating, requiring the mandatory servitude of others.

Tony rubbed his jaw and began pumping his foot. He listened as a mop bucket squeaked down the run. He wanted to see who was pushing it, to look at another face. He wondered if maybe they could get something going. Wouldn't somebody who's been around here know a thing or two? He cocked his head, and straightened as the sound grew nearer. "Hey!" he yelled. But all he could see was unfocused mesh. And all he could feel was pain. Already, he hated the turn around.

When they reopened the chow hall, later, the sun was nearly gone. Yet it was *hot*; red, purple, orange, leaking through an arm of finger-like clouds. It was as if a skin of some sort had been peeled from the horizon, exposing a series of bloodwork and veins. I scraped along the track, in the direction of my dorm, the taste of cheap boiled meat gristling up my throat. How long would it take the cops to blueprint a plan, a dome, to encase our prison and yard? I wanted that sky: it was this thing far away, screaming, changing. A kaleidoscope over our small, hard world.

I was ready to settle for that sky.

Steve Fisher

frenching spanish for cherry jean

Big red *beso*
flowering
in your mouth.

Rock Salt & Glissandos

weather nose

Winter
at midnight
in a late August
Arizona mountain wind

  —Encroaching
  —Off season

with nine pages
of calendar weight
left
till parole.

Steve Fisher

slam

At 30' fixated
on a dog's
head pasted to
a monument

gravity over
left shoulder
right left a
wicked
headache all
over like
extended brain
weight.

Rock Salt & Glissandos

monocraft

I'd say it probably is a bit different in jail, but—in or out—it also seems that the hardest thing to do is to put what you've experienced into an expression of your own, then equally hard to get that individuality past the forestylings of the overpopulas. I was having my share of trouble with the prison guards—*system* guards, really—but I realized that same type of resistance extended far into the world: as if certain people had a police line, built into their brain, their blood, their plasma. The court agencies—the probation officers and drug counselors in particular—were so lightweight in content and suggestion, in feeling and comprehension, that I thought of everyone—from the dust maidens to the form clerks—as a skinsucker, with a pudgy sort of vacancy. My balls recoiled at this pulseless, vibeless, neuro-social monobond, at the superficial depth toward superficial "issues," and at the ridicule and non-understanding I got from restrictive code-workers whose only ultimate belief was in the penal system. Charles Ives called these blowheads ROLLO in his time, scrawling the name far and wide through music scores and insurance memos. I did my *time*, raggedly thinking of this situation, raggedly aware, though at times I went off in exhilaration in a jail cell and only needed the one word: skinsucker.

I thought it was the perfect expression, but then I could have been out of my head.

At any rate, there was television, advertisement, macho chords for aftershave and pigtail jingles for diet-wear. The radio playing like a fishtrot, with stalk-slender flutes of persuasion. Billboards, slicks, Meese and Andy Rooney. The governor bought police with school money; with any money. Science and exploration, backcast to technology. The bread oven was replaced by microwave and the arbitrator was computer-margined. It was all there, like a trick bag in a wind trap. It was one of the first things I detoxed from back in County.

It didn't seem so long ago, as I cut through the prison yard to phone my woman, but I remembered the rote and routine and the rubber on tile of a year ago like yesterday. And the Swivel-Johnny's, trying to inquire me out, then conceptualize me on paper with a professional, useless, office-file vocabulary. So few people understood the trough and the monocraft of it, so few had taken a step back from *anything*. It was hardly a revelation, but it lay out before me, geometrically, something like a theater.

In the southwest yard area, near the pig farm and the vocational schools, the L-shaped prison dorms seem no taller than a table top. The rudimentary cut of high-windowed concrete, block set and *stationary*, make them look like toys; like something you'd quickly outgrow. They were blunt white objects, roofed with a salute pitch, hedged out with fern spacings and an adobe wall up front. The wall held a small section of dirt for flowers in the summer, similar to a gladiola playpen, but the Arizona mountains are cold in the winter and the old withering shoots were curled up now like laminate. Ice puddles would form in the dirt, but the halfwalls were popular hangouts. There sometimes wasn't much choice: sixty men lived down two short runs per dorm, jammed in like circus animals, wailing like an aviary.

I walked between these two dorms, named Bierson and Looper, to the halfwall. The only color on the dorm was a sort of basset-red door, which opened perpendicularly to the street from a sallyport. A foyer. It opened periodically, an arm knifing out with voices, the faces unseen from the phone booth.

"Sheit Rufus, I wooden even *tend* that ugly bitch!"

"I see ya baby; I SEE YO' PRIDE!"

The booth was one of those bygone street shacks, an inward collapsible without panes that rocked in one direction. But the blue, fiber-form security phone (collect calls only — no third party, no credit cards, no directory assistance) was BOLTED to a welded strength against that frame. Gang tight. Since you couldn't rip it out, I guess you either beat the phone or cart it off with the booth. But one of the better things about this penitentiary were the open-air phones. Inmates took beatings after conversations, overheard in a corridor.

It was cool out there, halfway up Mt. Graham, but the December sun hit like a spot heater, touching my face, sending my blood throughout. I wore my prison denims and T-shirt, with a flannel that was sleeved at the biceps. My chest warmed as I punched my girl's number, my head lifting up as I pulled in the clean winter air.

Well, she did have her faults, and I was nearing parole. She was accepting of platitudes, of tiny sounds that don't reach the floor from a sofa. Of stale ideas and membership drives. Of eggnog at Christmas and a car mechanic's word. She wanted to believe, almost too much, in a world of checkered tablecloths and shoes that were scuff-free. Of nice visits with mother on Sunday mornings. In the bulk feed that came from advice givers and co-workers.

But she also had a streak of curiosity and wonder, of hot foods and spice and cars that flashed chrome as they sped down the highway. It was a little something. She kept the place clean and wanted a home. I didn't argue with that. Kids, if my job application went through. She was quiet enough, never drunk, didn't touch drugs and left early in the morning for work. Qualities I appreciated. But she wavered against me at times, or she couldn't make up her mind about certain things and became futile, flustered, tense in the elbows. I clocked it as a monthly. Still, there was a delay that put a gap in her, as if she didn't understand me after six years of common-law marriage. My habit was to stay contemporary. I didn't want her lousing up my parole.

"Valley operator. Your name?"

"Yardfish."

I tapped my palm on the handbag ledge as the call went through. Saturday afternoon. State pen to metropolitan Tucson. We chatted a moment. Roommates. Then she seemed excited about some shit or other.

"Easy to be overwhelmed when there's not much offered to begin with," I said.

"You think it's ridiculous, don't you?" she snapped.

"I think it's a vacuum."

"Well, I think it's nice. They have two shows and serve drinks, and the waiters all wear hats."

"Baby balls."

"Just because *you* don't like it doesn't mean I can't."

"I just think it would be a waste of time."

"I think it's fun."

"I think it's a goofy fucking bland basin."

"Can't you just be accepting?"

"Shit, acceptance is the thing that leads to acceptable behavior. Acceptable behavior is only a sheen of dashboard music that narrows the odds for me."

Up the street came a swell of inmates, young white toughs with tats and bandannas. I was white too, only older. The courts could be very indiscriminate.

They *proceeded* toward me with their *attitude*, but the sound I heard was laughter, that of a kid wanting something good to eat.

"I suppose that means you won't go to A.A., either," she said.

"Not if I don't have to."

"Ooo Christ!"

"If they make me go I'll go," I told her, "but you know that I've been going here. Maybe I've learned something already."

"Well, at least that's good," she conceded.

They had the thing here twice a week. We went into near riot at the podium meets, over snitches and women, over the bastards who had burned us in drug deals. We howled and applauded as stories were told about cops who were decked in bar room brawls; about cops who were dead. But we joked and agreed that drinking might lead to disturbance at a simple burglary, or unwanted flourishes while writing a check. Especially risky to a car thief. We went and drank the free coffee. Heard that A.A. on the outside was like a roomful of bosses. Received credit for weekly attendance.

"Anyway," I said, "I have things to do. I can only allow for so much shit from the parole department and the infantile games of their agents and network. *And* their release programs. It would help us both if you found it in yourself to relax." I acknowledged the young men as they passed on the walkway, going up to the dorm. Someday they would have a similar conversation. Regardless of where we had been before, now we were on the same side—to a degree.

A flock of blackbirds woke up in a fir tree as they passed; squawking, rasping and shining in the branches. The limbs rolled like a conductor's baton in allegro ovals, then flapped in tempo as the birds sprung through the tree. I was trying to get through to her.

"They aren't going to *do* anything to you on parole," she rather bleated, "and some of this stuff might be good."

"You're light in the head!"

"Why can't you just go along with it?"

"Listen, they aren't there to potentiate or better me. They're around to snoop in, to become a voice against you at a later date. Idiot voices. Tongue welts. *Talkers.* Can't you understand?"

"What do you intend to do that you're so worried about?"

"Nothing." I flipped a smoke out and rolled it on my lip. The receiver warmed against my ear.

"Then you've got nothing to worry about."

"Little Jesus!"

I could see her sitting on the chair, at home in the front room, with her legs crossed and a finger twirling a strand of hair, the door open to the (phenotropic) sunshine that the Chamber of Commerce always pushed. Coach-car blouse and slacks. Barefoot. A cup of coffee—milk, no sugar—on the ice chest next to her. She had cursed the milk carton when she poured the last of it into the coffee. And now she dropped the hair from her finger to cradle her chin in her palm.

"Well?" she spasmed.

All her years in a single line across her forehead.

"I know you can't really understand all of it because you've never been in *this* system, but it's not unlike a pavilion at Disneyland or a compound equation or anything run *systematically.* Just that the stakes are higher, and what they can do—now that they've got you—is play this run of the self-perpetuating criminal and herd you down the plank. They have reams of laws that were written specifically for ex-cons, felonies only by definition of *language*— are you getting there?" I broke.

Rock Salt & Glissandos

"Sort of," she said almost evenly, trying to follow. And it was difficult to follow, not that difficult, but forty-eight hours of prison would surely cover the experience I was pushing on her through mere grammar.

"Okay. Now, about thirty percent of the laws pertain to offenses that a so-called reasonable person would find objectionable—I mean the heinous and horrid and repulsive shit the stuff that the newspapers go for. About twenty percent of the laws handle fines and probation for the business tribe, then a majority of the *remaining* fifty percent are trap laws for those with a record. For *me*."

"Why don't you just think positively," she quipped sequentially, sounding something like an inbred loudspeaker instruction.

"Because I don't have a cloud in my head and a cushion under my ass, that's why," I said. "You gotta realize that if I accidentally brush against someone it can be a crime of simple assault. Disorderly conduct or disturbing the peace if I play the stereo as loud as I'm gonna need it. If I enter the backyard of a friend, to see if he's home, an asinine provision of third degree burglary is available to enforcement."

"Come on," she coaxed, "they aren't going to do that. You're just overreacting."

"Shit, the prison takes in about four thousand people a year. *You* see about two hundred cases, maybe, which are covered in the news. I'm considered an industrial possession, a prison possession, someone they may try to get back. I'm their job security at this point, what they hope to be a so-called repeat offender— You can't be that dense, can you?" I asked.

"No, but if you're not doing anything wrong . . . I just don't understand why they'd charge you with burglary," she said, rubbing against the arm of the law.

"Simple. It's because the neighborhood *watch* groups and the snitches behind the curtain can't SEE what you're doing in a *back*yard."

"Oh Christ, you're still not doing anything wrong."

"Sure, that's just it. And it's not a question of doing anything *wrong*. It's a matter of *exposure*, all around. Being overheard or observed is the first mistake an ex-con can make. Anything could be construed or contrived from a footstep, just like any caption can be placed under a photograph. It's a helluva risk just buying a loaf of bread."

A soft rubbery voice came from nowhere.

"Want a light?"

I'd seen him before, always in a hooded, gray zip-up sweatshirt, smoking extra-length cigarettes. He had a cross-legged frailness and was high necked with bitch-brows in a tight, sharp face. A high tether of anger was strung through his voice. He was snit paced and box shouldered, hugging himself as he walked: a pink punk faggot; a pug tart. He was right next to me, outside the booth, ready to strike a match. I had less than a month to do.

"I'm on the phone, asshole," I told him.

Steve Fisher

"I just though' that—." He had a backlisp.
"Think it on someone somewhere else."

He did a swift pivot and scurried off, clasping himself before the bright arm of Looper; flip-nosed with a gray shadow wit. Someone over in classifications had provided him. I only thought of ironing boards and spray bottles.

I stared into the snow-covered mountains for a moment and shifted my weight on the warped floor of the phone booth. Two young petty fraud offenders, Shelly and Collins, stepped out of Looper, quietly talking, deep in conversation. They sat on the halfwall.

"Then what do you intend to do?" she barked in a screetch.
"Correspondence school." I said. "They can't deny me an education."
She clicked her tongue and groaned.
"What the hell's wrong with you?" I asked.
"That's not *work*," she spat, "That's not a *job!*"
"It's a lot of *effort*. Just what the fuck's a job supposed to be?"
"Work!"
"Hell, you're talking about a nightstick operation. I'm preparing for the next decade."

It seemed like the way to go, if I could get through all the paperwork and formalities. The Feds supplied grant money, so that was one end. I never went to school much beyond tenth grade, but I read plenty and some of my projects were similar to a college curriculum, so the other end was to find a school, one that I could receive credit from for what I already knew. Between the two ends was the shuck of performance, the thing that everyone, apparently, was trained to judge.

Of course, I knew what she was talking about. She meant that I should be applying myself around a conveyer belt or a housing start, or roped into a palm tree, one hundred feet above street level, clipping fronds as my neck wrenched and the parole officer looked on with guns in his head and the cuffs hanging from his belt loop. I was full of treble and drive and bloodpulse at this stage of my sentence, and thought I could get my grain with the right college instructor. But I had a low motivational threshold when it came to sucker work. Always. Always will.

"What about a job in a restaurant?" she pleaded. I could see the balls of her feet tapping the floor, as if she were foot-slapping a swirl of ants.

"I tried that once. I couldn't sell a berry."

"You're not going to get a job and you're going to sit around, and I'll end up supporting us!" Her voice kept pitching up in tone to calamity, to a measured self-righteous distress that I'd seen suctioned to many people who made between four and six dollars an hour, the kind of attitude that usually bought more laws and police than groceries. I took a hit off my cigarette and pulled in a huge cloud of unexpected smoke, as if the square were pressure-rigged.

She popped her tongue like a brat who was being forced to eat spinach

Rock Salt & Glissandos

with lemon.

"You only want two things from me," she snarled with a rush of hot underbreath.

"Well, maybe you can learn something else," I suggested rather broadly, a few things running through my mind.

"OOOO-O!" she wheezed. It was like getting a blizzard from a shower head. I spoke quickly.

"The thing to do is make an inversion of the situation, while at the same time giving them no reason to turn Soviet on me. That's all. If I'm in school they'll have virtually nothing to look at, nothing to implicate or indict me on, no way to hold my nut."

I paused and heard the fog or the connection. She was too much of a spendthrift not to be listening. I glanced at the fir tree, which was quiet and still but full of lazy blackbirds, then went on.

"The grant money available to me should cover rent and so forth, but the main thing is to stay low and go about my business without it becoming theirs. That way, things stand a chance of working out. Plus, if they try an' retro-act me, they'll come up empty handed."

"But you've got to *do* something."

"I've got to take care of *myself*, not the police operation or any of their salt. Isn't that enough?" I watched as the cigarette burned.

One of the wall sitters hopped down and strolled toward me. "Well, yeah . . ." she slowed. In fact, she changed her verbal footing as if she suddenly had dropped to timber elevation. "I just want things to go smoothly, so we can do stuff together. I don't like having to get you out of jail at four in the morning all the time."

"That's old," I said. "That's why I wanna do parole right. So I won't be back."

Without intruding, Shelly moved his hand out and gave me an up-nod. "Shorts?" he said softly. I gave the remainder of my cigarette to him. He and Collins passed it back and forth. But when Shelly inhaled it looked as though his ribs were being sucked up his throat with a sort of swollen effect.

"Okay," she said, "we'll see what happens. As long as you can make it work, I guess it's alright with me."

"Well shit, yeah," I said.

It reminded me of how my grandmother used to give in to what I was doing when I was a kid. She couldn't quite figure it out, but felt the need to convince herself that she had gotten the last approving word in.

"So it's ok?" she asked.

"I think it'll work."

Shelly and Collins were laughing over something.

"So what do you want to do when you get out?" she asked.

"I don't know. Go out and stand there for a moment, then start with all the rest."

"I've got a surprise for you. You're going to like it."
"Oh?"

I looked into the mountains as she talked on. There had been a recent snow, but the roads which had been cleared were sticking out like an iodine treatment. We were involved again. It was alright; it felt good.

I hung up and the bell popped on the phone. But the phones were rigged not to accept incoming calls, of course.

"Hey man," Collins nodded at me, "c'mere an' let me ask ya something."

Collins had a recent state haircut. It was a black mid-fall that shot down the back of his head like an oiled shingle. I loosened my shoulder blades as I stepped out of the phone booth, freeing myself in the air. Shelly looked on.

"When I'm fuckin' my girlfriend," he asked studiously, "don't I have to make her cum too?"

"Depends where you fuck her," I laughed, then cruised by the dorm, looking for something else.

It was easy to figure: I'd be out on the ninth of next month, which was only ten more days and a get-up. The state of Arizona would give me fifty dollars gate money to rebuild my life with, but I had something curbed and a ride home and a backer in Cal who worked as a college instructor. I knew people on all sides of Tucson now, including the Five Points (Robles Junction) area. I had a book to look up in the library by E. M. Cioran and enough civil rights to check it out, provided they had it. If it seemed as though I was going to flunk parole I figured I'd think of my out-time as a short pass. It could happen, because I was up and alive and in *motion*, while a slow social basting was being applied to the world, continuously, much like drippings on rotating beef. But I'd never let them catch me dirty. I had fourteen inch biceps like rock-solid steel and a year's worth of horsepaste. The garage groups I liked were playing on the radio every Friday night. The earth curved just right if you could see it from a distance—we were only gliding through space, after all. Things could certainly work out right.

I walked across the yard, concentrating on the feeling in my feet as they moved cleanly through my shoes. It wouldn't be long now.

Rock Salt & Glissandos

short steps to another world

He slowly began losing his hell-sweat accuracy
and park bench wine-wit
after years with a "winning team" company
that provided no benefits no health insurance;
his bones were a torturing ash-frail grade
teeth chipping like saltines
a few recollections like tapeworms in his withering head plumes —

but his infrequent five-day blackout drunks
were still loaded with snarling verbal sniper attack
beautiful, at times,
only now he spoke in disconnected slats
as if troubled by face-flies
or a hot solder head-stitch.

At fifty five he was decked
and quickly growing old on a saliva-thin pension,
the neighboring world now a punched-out tin wrap
as a kid across the way laced his cleats for a pick-up game —
growing old and forgotten like back roads
that were finally narrowed useless by erosion.

But the blackouts and drinking carried him through
once a month when the check came, kept him somehow circulating
tho revoking the rest of his days
that were spent strained and coiled in a room like a mop bucket —

but the graveyards deserved believers first, all the denominated
all the cash customers —

but in my judgment his checks should come weekly with
a collated overlay which
brings a world *forth*
instead of leaving a cracked old man growing walnuts in his head.

Steve Fisher

pitchfork standing flame
& time crap filaments

Time is an excuse you taught, and sadly I borrowed
your pitiful dormitory of
   play logs and domestic tickets,
erratically stashed like crystals in ice wafers—
   in your headbone in
   your mulch in your rat frame
   your secretions
your train of ways.

   I was sitting simply
in a pouch you called a chair
   that night,
   timed to a phonetic hunk
   of apologetic resistance
as you stood listening

   —room center,
   calm—

though a dozen you's
   circulated
the room snapping
invisible filament whispers—

   CRAP!
   CRAP!
   CRAP!

as I lingered through,
setting my first emotional
honesty up
in ages,
merely a kneeling trite
   asphyxiate

Rock Salt & Glissandos

to your Highness I
now call DOXY
with moistened lips.

Steve Fisher

slowtime in the jailhouse

Time goes slow so we play cards and talk to each other:
   What you do if you don't drink, then Al?
   Eat my girlfriend's pussy.
   Hell, I saw her on 5th. Eat her pussy more than five minutes
                         and you join the navy.
Shit . . .

At first time is fire. It is the backside of the fast emotion you feel
as a kid on Christmas. Then it fades into folds,
hanging like tread from a landlady's neck.
   Hey Fisher, I thought we was goin' fishin'.
   We'll drag Lake Mead for your brains, Salvetez.
   What it is Fisher.

Time is longer inside because there's little distortion. The senses
                                       are raincoated
with little exit to large life. Hector shuffles the deck
and teaches me rummy. Mondo passes a cigarette. Neither
is pain and I accept both.

Rock Salt & Glissandos

electric latches

Things tensed up more than usual in the camp when rumors of a shakedown were confirmed. In the first place, your stuff wasn't guaranteed to be safe, just because you found a nook to stash it in. Everyone in the joint was thinking of the remote, obscure, nearly sub-prison regions of the yard, and there weren't that many spots available: the yard was just a small dirt tundra, level as a municipal airstrip and anybody could get to your shit fairly easy. Secondly, the routine structure of the institution got knocked around and jammed *inward*, to where we live — this meddling with and confiscation of our possessions — so there was anticipation and complete sensing of the dirty little grub violations about to come down. It made some people ugly, others noncommittal. It affected everyone in degrees. It became the sole topic on the yard, starting a week before they came through.
"Big shakedown coming up next week, Holmes."
"Ain't it a bitch?" — or —
"Say man, wanna buy a pair of Levi's cheap?"
"Shit, they're just gonna steal 'em if I have 'em laying around the house."
"You can wear them no problem."
"Except they'll be looking at our property receipts."
"Alright, then lemme get a smoke offa ya."
"Don't have none."
But as the customer walked off, without upping one, he felt the eyes of the peddler upon him like a hot coating glaze so he turned around, looked at the guy, yelled "Fuck your goddamn Levi's!" to take a bit of the heat off himself. Very quickly another system had been developed by the population, just to accommodate the bullshit. But I can't help thinking that what is supplied to adapt to in our prisons is the same thing, in attitude, that will *aggravate* a man's sentence and get him more time before a judge, until the man feels like

77

Steve Fisher

he's lost in a carnival of mirrors.

What *I* needed, at any rate, was to find a trusty. Or a dry place somewhere, inside of a building. The problem was that most of the complex buildings were housing units, "dorms," and I had bulk that couldn't be buried outside. Books, magazines, a few personal papers. I was leaning against my locker, looking at the brown crotch of earth that hardened outside of my window, thinking *the library*. It could work. It could be a solution. I could pattern my books along the shelves with the others, and pick them up after the police swept through. A dust devil suddenly whirled up from the ravine in the road, and ran toward my window like a powdered tan skirt. It was large, violent — a twisting spike of cone. I slid my small, glass windowpane along, before it crashed through the screen and showered all over my bed and the rest of the cramped, double cell.

I turned away from the locker, stuck my hands in my pockets for something to do. Actually, there was a chill in the air. The dorm was pale and stuffy and I stood there, breathing, thinking just who had what type of jacket out of the twenty-five people I was routinely locked down with: Shorty, Flame-out, Pinky, and Spider were all doing time for burglary. Igor and Butter-butt, along with Manther and Blood Bath, had long time for either manslaughters or murder. We had Big Al (#1, white) and Big Al (#2, black), doing old-code time with Tombstone, Rebel, Barbershop, and High Tower for various forms of armed robbery. Both Rolly and Hammer had picked up their numbers for boosting. The Torch had arson and escape on his jacket, with some minor raps of D&D. Also theft. He'd never see minimum security. Neither would Mad Dog, or M&O, who totaled between them four hundred years. Aggravated battery with kidnapping and burglary. *Judicial* winter. Five others suffered these walls for rather personal, non-criminal offenses, primarily the use of drugs. Like me. Chickenshit but profitable for the new penal code, to be sure. And that left Wanda, whose real name was Warren, but Butter-butt figured it sounded more natural, more masculine, to be punking a Wanda because you say "Warren" and motherfuckers take it that you got tendencies as well: just a matter of formality, a language, pride—though my ideas about it were more straightforward than that. But regardless of the circumstances that brought people down, the material to stash was about the same: utilitarian. I knew all of these convicts well enough that at night, in the semi-darkness, I recognized each one by his leg strides and footsteps.

It was M&O who came up to my cube. He was short. Young. Athletic. With corn rows. And some sort of silver bead woven through his hair. The designer shades he constantly wore were blacker than silk screen, but he contrasted little to the function of the dorm: body drag, mere complaisancy, combined in a listless May afternoon. He always hit on you for something.

"Ya don't have no *Choco*late Twins?" he asked me.

"No candy, no sweets," I told him, but he looked at me for an instant longer than expected. I said, "There's just no way to rely on that dentist around here.

Rock Salt & Glissandos

You get a cavity, they'll clean your teeth with shaving stones."

I looked at him with the feeling, and thought (it was a personal thing) of someone enlarging their vision to the circumference of a ferris wheel.

"I hears that," said M&O, as a flurry of voices shucked through the corridor from the entrance way at the top of the run. There was a beef of some sort which I knew nothing about, nor cared to participate in, so I just fixated the sound into a jazz of overall commentary. It caught M&O, too. He pepped his head up, looking over at the door to see his homeboys in dispute. He wandered off with his *purpose* and got up there with them, prepared to get down.

But these little skirmishes went on all the time, nearly everywhere. It was hardly anything new. Sometimes it resulted in blood, but to me it was yet another thing to endure: simply by preferring to contribute to myself, and not to the hordes. It could be rough enough just maintaining that. But I hardly gave a fuck about what was stipulated by expectation—from either the courts, who anticipated the self-perpetuating criminal, or by the convicts who only played it in one strict way. I just did my time as would a dolphin among a sea of deadly creatures.

As the warden would say, I didn't measure up. Hardcore, *ése*, hardcore.

I rubbed my back against the wood of the locker, thinking it might take a couple of trips to move my books through the library turnstile. Of course the cops were up there, security—the thing which prevented me from doing it myself—but anyone who worked there could carry a load of overdue books in. They did it all the time. I couldn't foresee any exceptional problems. I listened to the whirring of Manther's tattoo gun, a few houses down from me. In a few days, the ream of authority would bear down and rip up the yard. I wanted to get on with it. I looked around.

M&O had moved off, somewhere, with his pals. The argument was traveling through our cold, concrete tombs to another wing, another house—to another multiplication—and very little traffic was moving on the ramp. Really, it was kind of peaceful: there were just six people over at Manther's, watching as he tattooed someone's ankle. But as Rolly got up and walked down the aisle I began thinking: this motherfucker can help clear the gate for me. Rolly had been transferred in recently, but I knew him all the way back to my jailhouse days in Tucson.

I said, "Rolly. You're a trusty up in the library now?"

He said, "Yes," very sharp and succinctly, intoning a wave through the word like he was riding on it. I'd always appreciated the manner in which he did time.

"You wanna do a little job for me?" I asked.

"Well, of course it depends," he said. We were eye-height on each other. His brown hair was still full, even though he was no longer a youngster.

"It's real simple. All I need is for you to take my books up to the library before this hoe-down next week. I can stash them, once they're through security."

He asked, "What's the load look like?"

I pulled a door open on my locker. They were already bagged up.

"Both of these bags," I said. "That's it."

Rolly just worked an eyebrow, beaming and present at the tip of my cube, then said, as a statement, "Books really scare them." He put a hand on top of my cube's ledge, eyes lit.

So I grinned back and told him, "Content in *any* form, really. I've noticed how they keep locking up these yard lawyers, the ones that make headway and get folks released."

"Sure enough."

"But I also know what you mean about books. They must only carry romance and science fiction on purpose."

"I'm telling ya," he said. "It's a big fucking joke up there."

"If you got the balls for that sort of laughter," I told him, but Rolly knew his way around and laughed along with me. As it slapped the walls in our nearly empty strip of housing, I thought, for an instant—it was really something like flashboard—of two small bombs going off in a quiet office.

"Hey! Keep it down over there!" someone shouted.

Rolly turned his head toward Manther's house, where a young fish was sitting around. The fish only wanted to cut in. Rolly turned his head back, nodding to me that it was nothing: nothing, except somebody was always pushing in.

I opened up my window again.

"Anyway," said Rolly, "if you want to lug one of those bags for me I'm starting my shift in half an hour."

"Alright," I said.

"I'll get them through with my other crap. Just a few things, not much."

"I'll be looking out my window," I nodded, "ready for you."

Rolly walked off and I sat down, on my bed. We were under such heavy procedure and security that most people, like Rolly, sensed the value of immediacy in a situation. Even the lames on the yard understood this, in their own way, mainly among themselves. It was the *attitude* which got things done. And, in large part, prevented folks from going to lockdown. Or street court. For mostly non-offensive, in-house charges, which the administration compounded into statistics for even more of the State's money.

I lit a cigarette and got the books from my locker, the grocery bags, and moved them to the bed. It was Saturday, and people began returning from visitation. It got crowded. Noisy. Convicts from all over the yard tripped through, some looking for friends, others casing houses, a good many of them hunting the dope bags which came in. Drugs were common in prison. Not only did they make people feel better, they altered perimeters within the Correctional ethic of time: a dull, dragging clock, defined by the repetition of daily events. But drugs created a freedom from these chains which hung about, everywhere, like so many links to a policy manual. Whites, blacks,

Rock Salt & Glissandos

Mexican, it didn't matter. Fifty people came through within twenty minutes, hustling, jiving, stretching an angle to the fine point of contact. The bullshit interlaced. By the time Rolly returned and said, "Let's jam," the dorm had become tight. Become grainy. It felt like I was being suctioned with attachments and I wanted to pull them off, but it was difficult—nearly impossible—something like flexing your own teeth. There had to be a better way to do really close-up time like this, I thought. Really, there had to be.

Rolly grabbed a bag. I grabbed a bag.

We then headed out.

The yard was scattered with inmates, a few cops. Smoke from the Sweat Lodge oiled the air. The Indians sat out there in a hut beyond the inside fence and sweated, we're told, as part of their spiritual practice. Fine. I got along with the Chiefs like a regular, but today, for some reason, their coals put out a hot, sardine stink. I don't know if I was simply unschooled in this ritual, or if the guards had exchanged logs as a prank—it really smelled of their mentality and underbrain—but I ingested it as yet another sign of forewarning. The stink blew heavily across the tract with the wind, and sheets of dust flew like bedding discarded in an alleyway. Not only did it darken the complex like an L.A. smog, it plated on the skin and redirectioned the senses as if, suddenly, you were stumbling drunk. I was familiar with the feeling. Rolly knew the feeling. Halfway across the yard he told me, "Back in Tucson, people stand out in the street and *point* when they see a cloud going over. They couldn't begin to imagine it down here."

"This really isn't weather," I'd already decided, "it's interrogation."

We moved onward, thinking about it, bucking our flesh against the overswelling gusts. I with one bag, he the other. Folded inside he had another bag with his own stuff. On both bags were other bags, ones we had fitted over the top as lids. All Rolly had to do was take both of them through the gate.

He said, "If you really want to put these on the shelf, get a pass for tonight and I'll leave them out. But they'll be safer if I just stash them in the cabinet."

"Alright," I said.

"If the librarian saw them sitting around, she might react and write up an incident report and turn them in.

"I've seen her," I said. "Let's just go with the cabinet."

He said, "Ehhh, buddy," with an inflection of parody, as we came to the side of a building by the gun tower. The gate. We stopped for a second, so I could hand him the books.

"No charge," said Rolly, "since we go back and were once tight."

I said, "You motherfuckers are making a fortune off this deal anyway. Good time to be a trusty, no doubt."

"We have stuff up there in the library," he said, "damn near looks like we went through the houses, vacuuming up essentials."

"You be *stylin'*, I'm sure."

"It's high season," he grinned, "what the fuck?" He then rounded the corner with the two bags, just like he'd heisted a couple of watermelons from a supermarket display. But I had confidence that I'd see them again: there were some people you just had to believe in.

I put my head down and started back through the yard, the desert cracking whip lines around my eyes, across my forehead. There were moments when I enjoyed the dorm, but usually I had to make it work, for me, because not only was I slow at times, I had the extra burden of being stupid: jokes went by I didn't understand, or the food that was fought over I couldn't stomach anyway. And much of the hair on the loud music seemed groomed, brushed, uncoiled, thin. Maybe that was just me. But I was in there so often, there at the center, feeling such tension in the air that my skin felt like vomiting. That's the only way to say it. There's an energy in reverse, it seems, that just suits up upon itself, then hangs on you like dry wall. Mother. *Never* get caught. I walked along and squinted, looking down as the dust broke from ripples to waves. It gritted on my teeth like dirty linoleum tile. But, for it all, for all the faces that howled from within this iron setup, I sometimes reasoned I had a jump of my own: I felt like a lightning bolt between beehives of grand symphony-reeling, striking, advancing to something above and beyond the walls, something which made me neither blood thirsty nor elite. As I looked up at the dorm, five young Mexicans were running from a dust devil. They danced with a waving of ball caps, knees kicking up, like it was some sort of ritual music from home.

I could only see them, unable to hear their giggling as I walked. That wind finally helped. Then, I was in.

> Leather soles scuffing concrete.
> Bones cracking in the joint.
> Humming tubes of artificial light.
> Red eyes, glazed, wondering.

Then corridor-length conversation. I heard locker panels slamming, wood on wood, metal on metal as the air vent was fitted together. Cups dropped. Towels snapped. Water ran loudly down the sink, unattended, as a lone giraffe gargled in my dreams. Windows scooted open, closed, as some of the blacks ran up and down the aisle. The two in the cube across from me sat waiting, on the hips of their beds, anticipating. I lifted, then dropped my eyelids.

The dorm began buzzing with hoots, nerves, hyperactivity. Uncirculating blood pulsed in the fingertips. I opened my eyes as M&O went past, shirtless and swaggering, making sounds like he had a locomotive in his chest cavity. I managed to roll over but I had a roommate who said, "Ill-mannered little fucker," and we left it at that.

It was too fucking early in the morning for me. I felt like I was waking with sinus cancer, whatever time it was, but as I reached for a cigarette I heard a brownsuit commanding, "BREAKFAST IN FIVE MINUTES. YOU WILL

Rock Salt & Glissandos

THEN RETURN TO YOUR HOUSING UNIT UNTIL SUCH TIME AS THE SHAKEDOWN TEAM ARRIVES. YOU WILL BE SECURED IN YOUR UNITS."

I peeked over the top of my cube's ledge. I wanted to make sure I got it right.

Sure enough, the old throat giving orders was just an administrative sergeant, nobody we'd ever seen before. So instead of possible questions, she received nothing more than a push-off.

"GIT ON OUT OF HERE, YA STINKY OLD WHORE!"

"YA DOUCHE WITH MEXICAN TAP WATER, SARGE!"

She said, "WE *WILL* COME THROUGH HERE, ANY WAY YOU WANT IT. ORDERS ARE IN EFFECT FOR TODAY."

"YA OLD *BUFFALO* HUNTER!"

She pushed out the door, locking it behind her. Half a dozen lacquered faces stood with her, some in the guards' cage, looking down the run at us. They mingled like ticket holders at a ballgame, only stiffly. One of them, one big greasy slob, wore a helmet with a face shield and carried a shotgun. I thought—he's on the payroll to make sure I don't read. I lay back down and lit up a tailor, as conversations splintered woodenly, numbing.

Then two things dawned on me that helped explain the dorm's jitters: not only was the Sarge's voice an unknown, it was *Monday*, not Wednesday, and Monday wasn't anticipated. Strange, though, because I knew most people were ready. As the nicotine absorbed in my blood I just lay there, not understanding the dimensional shock. Rolly went by and I asked, "What time is it?"

"Not even six," he said. I heard him lighting a cigarette next to me in his cube.

That's another thing, I thought. Some of us never get up until noon, including me. I reasoned that mornings were an active write-up shift, and my strategy was to skate as much as possible. I was thinking of minimum, of the streets. But it wasn't even six o'clock yet. No wonder people were already feeling hammered, beat. Across from me, sunken in the concrete above my neighbor's locker, the small-barred window looked like lips peeled back and affixed with a shine. This was sun, the beginning of morning.

Rolly poked his head around, looking into my cube. I drew again on my cigarette.

"Get your ass up and do *time*," he told me, but the look on his face wasn't a challenge.

I exhaled in his direction. This shit of waking up was pointless.

"You want to hear some facts?" he asked me.

"Go ahead. I'm nothing but earcone."

"Alright," he smiled, "they're shaking the other houses down before us. That's three hundred people. They won't even be here till late afternoon. Also, M&O's on the way out, along with one of his buddies. Cops are gonna roll 'em up during breakfast."

Steve Fisher

Rolly dragged casually on his cigarette, gripping it between his forefinger and thumb. I now had the facts.

I said, "Serves the little prick right. These cretins are coming through to abuse us, and he thinks we're having a party."

Just as I said that, M&O walked by. As he bent down to whisper something to my neighbor I saw the muscles—traps—expand in his neck.

"So fuck 'im," I said.

"Yeah," said Rolly, "I agree. So do most of the people on the run."

"It's a complicated kindergarten," I said, "but I've noticed. And maybe now, since we've got all day, I'll stretch my shit out and go back to sleep."

"Let's go to breakfast, long as we're up," he said. "Hey, why not?"

I agreed.

I sat up, yawned, took a last hit on my cigarette then tapped it out in the ashtray. It was good having someone like Rolly around, someone who understood the caravan much in the manner that I did: most of it was toss-off. I slipped my rough state jeans on, feeling them crease into my skin. I thought, it's not just these pants: the whole fucking dorm is like wearing an overcoat, an old stuffy overcoat that's too tight in the sleeves. But not only was that my main problem, others, by their reactions, by the things they said and the webs in their eyes, stated as much in a sort of absence. Rolly and I went in and ate the eggwhip. It was tasteless, oversalted and grayish, like the clouds.

It was fucking hot coming back from the chow hall. It was always hot out there, but the wind hadn't yet picked up. It would. It wouldn't help. Spider, walking a step or two ahead of us, hacked up a loogie and spit it in the dirt. But as we cleared the side of the chowhall and came into the yard, the first thing we saw were cops. Outsiders. Their special fucking scavenger crew, brought in as a "service patrol." They were milling around our dorm, twenty or so, some of them going in and out. Vigorously. Carelessly. But oh so *importantly*. An old white pickup truck was parked outside on the walk.

"Change of plan," said Rolly. "Looks like we're first."

"What the fuck?" asked Spider.

"I'll bet when M&O brought the heat, they got in and decided to stay," I said.

"Yes," said Rolly, slowing up and lighting a cigarette. "They figured, 'Why lug the team around when we're already here?'"

"That mu-ther-fucker," said Spider. "I've still got some shit in my locker."

"Better get it now," said Rolly, "before they crawl up our ass with a flashlight."

As Spider hurried off, a call came over the loudspeaker: "TENSION ON THE YARDS-ards-ards. ALL RESIDENTS OF HOUSE FOUR REPORT TO YOUR UNIT ASAP!" and we did, since we had no other place to go. Rolly said, "I know they can't touch me," and while I also thought it was true for myself, I didn't at all like the idea of them shuffling through my cube. Getting in close, under the guise of security. I took a pull off of Rolly's cigarette as we

84

walked, scraping my lungs like I was choking down hot bricks. It was still too early in the morning for me.

Spider had made it in, but the cops were all over. In the dayroom, the guards' cage, pitter-pattering along the ramp. Three of them were at M&O's, going through his stuff. M&O stood quietly (for a change) and watched, trying to look bad: the expression on his lips said, "Wha' th' *fuck* man, wha' th' *fuck!*" but to me it really looked more like exertion. Nobody bothered to ask him what it was all about. Nobody got close to him at all.

His shit was boxed up and wheeled out the door. They led him down the ramp, shirtless but freehanded, only now they had his sunglasses. His character. But just as they escorted him out the door, six cops stormed through like precinct rookies. Like cadets, practicing for a house raid. Why? What was the exhibition all about? Others followed, as the first ones lined up against the wall. I turned and noticed a young Mexican up the run, looking nervous, antsy, fidgeting in his cube. The Torch, right next to Spider. But really, just standing there with that *look*. I thought the best thing to do was simply lie down and twiddle my thumbs, so I did.

"GENTLEMEN, EVERYONE STAND AT THE FOOT OF YOUR BED. WE'LL BE INSPECTING YOUR HOUSES AS SOON AS YOU'RE COUNTED. YOUR COOPERATION WILL SPEED THIS ENTIRE PROCEDURE ALONG."

Bastards. I stood at the foot of my bed and was counted. Then I sat down, waiting.

They came inspecting, all right, but now each one of them had a partner. A woman. One of the female "counselors" from the Administration building, who had also put in for this shift: the counselors would get double-time pay from their supervisors, because the supervisors ranked this as "hazardous duty." Some scam. Most of them, like the others, we didn't even know. Our own fucking counselors. But instead of adding a softer, feminine border to the touch of Statehood, they clawed at our quarters like leopards after jungle meat. Starting with the first house, first cube, first party on the count sheet.

"Take everything out of your locker and put it on your bed, and I mean *every*thing," she told Spider. Loudly, coarse. "Clothes, towel, books, radio, tapes, Bible. Legal papers. I want to see your folders." She scanned a checklist, up close with her pen, brown tassels of pageant hair flying. But her skin was the texture of old foam. I noticed the young one, the one who stood next to her.

"Shaving kit and personal hygiene effects," she continued. "I want to see your number etched on your reading lamp, radio . . . and I guess you don't have a television here. Stationery supplies are now limited to one notebook and a box of envelopes. I want to see them *now*."

She was standing over Spider at the foot of his bed, while her partner crowded the cube. Just staring. Supervising. Watching each move that he made. Behind his cube stood the slob with the shotgun. The cop in Spider's house said to his partner, "This guy's got five pairs of socks, Lilly. Aren't socks a limited item?"

The dorm was suddenly quiet. My ears rang a little.

Lilly moved in, checking her list. She brushed against the cop for a moment, almost like they were nuzzling. They looked crude together. I saw them, glaring, over fed. "The provision calls for three pairs. I'll start making a pile for his box of disallowables," she said, and I, at that point, sickened by their grayness, pictured two rats fucking in the trash behind the State House, atop a discarded copy of the Arizona Revised Statutes.

Title 31.

Rolly looked in over the top of my cell ledge. "If she was born counting, she'd still be in single digits," he said. I laughed no problem, but I also remembered my writing board. It was big enough that I could place it on a box and have a table, but small enough that I could hold it in my lap and make a portable out of it. But it was contraband. Their policy against writing materials. I slipped my board on a special, convict-designed rail at the top of my bottom locker, fitting it flush so it would only feel like a piece of unfinished wood.

The agents, cops, counselors wandered around, ransacking the cubes in a spirit of duty. Lord. *Close up time*. I felt I was resisting a colony of moles while being packed down under, down in the earth, but I forgot about that when they got to my cube. They also hit my neighbors, Tombstone and Pinky. My cellmate as well. The first thing I sensed was that they felt comfort from the whole thing.

"Open your locker for us, will you?" asked the girl, the same girl I had watched near Spider's. "This won't take very long."

"Spread your things out on the bed, Sir," said the cop.

He was young but seemed tight, inflexible, braided like a wire cable. Mustache-trim, polished. The girl just looked like a Mexican teenybopper, Americanized but sexy in these slick, gray pants. Pure bone mama. I started by pulling my few clothes out.

Then the cop said, pointing, "What about those cassette tapes? You have property receipts for those tapes?"

"Sure," I said, but as I looked through my file of papers I could only find six receipts. I had a total of twelve tapes, actually, that had come through the mail and were legally on my books.

The cop said, "Juanita, mark down on his inventory sheet an inventory of six tapes. Sir, the others are contraband."

"Now, wait just a minute," I said.

"All items that can't be documented, we consider contraband," he said.

He became adamant about his argument, log rolling, but the bulk of it was so far down in the lower-human register I couldn't distinguish it from dog fat. Juanita placed my tapes in a box, then he got in my locker and began pulling things out. Pencils, paper, a bottle of white-out. Not as if he owned them, himself, but almost like the function of my shit was for a mutual welfare, a welfare I wasn't even part of. I was losing out to the proportion of some ill-sided equation and it was apparent, now, to us all.

"Juanita, this pencil sharpener? This eraser?"

But it wasn't like they were merely playing trivia with my stuff, and I would lose some tapes with other small, but important items. That, in fact, happened to everyone, daily. It was more just a matter of watching—up close—as they worked every surface and diameter of my household, that I realized exactly what it all meant: that power is simply the formality of disregard. Here, in my locker. Out, in the streets. Time and again we suffer the fools, the subordinate, the weary definition of predominance: a highly formulated racket, I thought; self-replicating but rather padded in the forehead. There was nothing to do but let them go at it.

As I hung around, effectively *in absentia* (the feeling was that of being outside this strange scratch of human netting), I watched Juanita's ass work those haunch-round, snug corduroys. Mmm, looked good, looked good to the entire run, but my mind skipped to other times, other places, other women I had seen. The dorm was cramping with minion heat but there was someone, a woman, not only of form and figure, but a dance which precedes the motion of her body. Eyes sparkling, with the tenor of simple being. Simple beauty. Glowing within her rhythms so warmly that you connect fully—completely—as if her mind and flesh were electric latches: a thing of the sun, of mercy. Of light spreading across a midwest cornfield in early July harvest give this to me once, Lord, before I die, and our negotiations will begin even once more: just someone who smiles from the guts of joy. That'll work. But not these servile attendants prowling the dorm, these faces of rain I lift away from. Let's settle someday, but someday as in soon.

I was drifting, Holmes, drifting. A big shakedown, and I was drifting.

Then the box patrol came in and dollied out a load of our belongings to the truck. I returned, watching. That truck would be making more than one trip, no question about it. Outside, we listened as the old engine turned over. It circulated, it roared. The cop waited. But Juanita and her partner seemed to be backing off now. Slowly, bit by bit.

They were nearly finished with my house, but Tombstone had enough stuff to keep the pair working his place for another hour. Or so it seemed, the way he was making a *point* out of every worn item he owned. Rolly had sailed through, but it didn't surprise me since he had just gotten here. "I know they can't touch me," he had said earlier, and I now laughed because it was his idea of a joke. Spider watched the run from his bed, also through. Even Juanita just sort of lolled around.

But the Mexican up from Spider, The Torch, looked even more self-cornered than when he'd stood there with *the look*. He was figuring that the cops had him, I believed, by the element of surprise. He almost looked stunned. Goddamn, I thought, whatever it is.

"Will these men be issued a sack lunch?" the cop at my bed suddenly asked Juanita.

"Yes," she said. "Promptly at thirteen hundred hours."

Shit, I thought, a sack lunch, as exhaust from the pickup idled in from the yard. A cop started yelling, "Cut the air on in here! Jesus, my lungs!"

Another cop, who'd been drifting the door by the shotgun, went out and flicked the switch. The vents buckled and the air shot out — cool, it felt good — but a rattling sound vibrated overhead at The Torch's. The Torch stood in his cube and bleached lighter than his skin color, his right hand shaking like he was salting an ear of corn. Goddamn, I thought, *be* convict. It's the last active right you'll be given until the graveyard.

"CELL SIXTEEN!" shouted one of the cops, and their whole fucking aggregate, like mules, clopped over. The cop who had yelled just pointed at the air vent, wrist up, like he'd been specially instructed on the application of that finger.

"Up here," he said. "Somebody get a screwdriver."

As everyone watched the grill come off, Rolly reached over and grabbed the tapes from my box. My box of contraband items. I said nothing, but started realizing how useful boosting skills could be.

"I think I've got it," said the cop. He was standing on Torch's bed, hand jammed into the vent.

"Here it is," he said, everyone looking.

But all he had was a cassette player, and as he pulled it from the vent the cord snagged on a piece of the fitted metal. It gave way, snapping to his cheek.

"AH-HA!" he said. A few people started laughing.

The cops milled for a second, rubbing flares of uniform on each other before walking back to our cubes. It was up to the loud cop, apparently, to decide if the deck was a matter of incident. But since he'd have to figure out who'd stashed it, regardless of The Torch's giveaway, the problem for the run was: Would he lie? We wouldn't find out for weeks, until the paperwork could be neatly arranged.

"I think we're about done here," the cop said to me, to Juanita, as they came back to my cell. He stood tall in my cube, masterful in the program of physical intimidation. "Check his contraband against your list. Let's make sure we get that list right before we go."

He put his hands on his hips and turned, looking down the run. Manther was across the ramp at a three-house distance, eyeing The Torch. Juanita sat on the bed and dug into my contraband box, my "excess" clothes, pencils, white-out, etc. She tossed them around with a peculiar sort of aversion, plowing her ass in my bed. Then she said, "Hey!"

The cop looked over, looked down at Juanita.

"I can't find his tapes," she said. She lowered her voice, saying sternly, "*His cassette tapes are missing!*"

Rock Salt & Glissandos

The cop looked at me with scorn. With seething, almost parental anger. I had nothing to volunteer.

"You're certain?" he asked her.

"They're gone," she said.

He glared at me a second longer, telling her: "Take the other ones—just for starters."

"I've got paper on those in triplicate around the yard," I said. "If you want to fuck with 'em, I'll take it up to the Major."

"Then where are they?" he asked. Both of them were staring.

"Search me," I said. I looked at them, looked back. "You're responsible. *You've* taken custody."

"Unless you stole them," he said, "which seems more than likely to me. I can file the appropriate charges on you, if I want."

I pictured him seated at a corner table in the bar, expressionless, laying it all out incrementally to his pals. Somebody else would be buying.

"If you wanna put the *buff* on this deal, you're entitled," I said. And that's all I said.

He paused, then told Juanita, "Check his locker. Maybe he put them back in."

She leaned into the thing, wriggling her young tail and pushing my stuff around. I noticed Spider looking her over from the top of the run. Juanita came up empty handed.

"He's a clever one," she said.

"Let's go," said the cop. But he told me: "Remember, I'll be watching you." I didn't think that was any news at all, so I watched them leave without saying a word. Juanita toted my box.

I stood up and opened the window. The earth I saw stretched for miles. Fruitless, still, crusted in bronze. The hot morning air came slowly through the grate, but I felt it loosening up my cell. Juanita had been right: it didn't take long for them to paw through.

They all filed out, soon after that. People moved around again, going from cell to cell. As I figured, Tombstone's house was the one that took the longest. Rolly came over and I pulled out the smokes.

"Good work," I said. "They won't be back."

"Probably not," he said, "but they'll always be around."

I said, "Yeah, there's a trick to that part."

"Naturally," he said, then he looked over at my roommate. In a sense, I hadn't been totally around. I really hadn't noticed him. I handed him a Camel filter, lit all of us up.

"Well," Rolly asked him, "did they cut your action back at all?"

"Naw," he said, "but you know what? It was kinda like having a dormful of M&O's running around . . . bunch of ignorant motherfuckers."

"Well, at least *he's* gone," said Rolly. "That only leaves about how many more?"

"Thing is," my cellie went on, "this is only a state joint. Half the people are in for real stupid, bungled shit, and the others ain't really done nothin at all. They put these mixtures in, like Manther and The Torch. You heard 'em earlier, right? Manther knew that The Torch stole his radio, but he couldn't prove it. Said he'd tear him a new asshole, though, if he ever found out. That was this morning."

"I was asleep," I said.

"Yeah. Well, that Torch has seen what Manther can do to a motherfucker. He's scared. And now the cops got the deck. I've been sitting here, just watching Manther shoot his eyes down the ramp. It's gonna get hot in here before the day's over. Count on it."

"What time you say it was?" I asked Rolly.

"8:39. We'll be locked down all day," he said.

"Anyway," said my cellie, "my point is that these stupid convicts in these state joints get themselves killed over nothin. Lots of them do. There's only about twenty-percent smart con in these state joints. But the real smart cons, the money makers, the stock market and extortion dudes, all of them's in the Federal pens. If you wanna be smart next time, cover your ass with a little mail fraud. That's what I'm gonna do. Then if the state comes up and beefs you for somethin, you only gotta snitch yourself off to the Feds. An' shit, they pick up your state time and run it C.C. No more of these Torch idiots. Or M&O's, for that matter. You got a way to get around in there."

"Almost sounds good," I said.

"If ya learn nothin else here, just remember my advice," he said. "Know why it only took an hour for this shakedown? State joints are impoverished!"

"*Sassing me, motherfucker?*" came a voice off the ramp, one of many we'd hear all day long. I had learned how to cup my ears, from the inside when I wanted, when I needed to block it away.

Like now.

Spider walked down, hyper, a bit rattled. Maybe they had gotten to his shit. I didn't ask, but he usually tried to dodge them with a smoke of Christianity. It was his only real hustle, but he never seemed to get far with it. He only seemed, really, to get more mixed up. I was leaning back against the wall, smoking with Rolly. Tombstone glanced at Spider from across the run.

"See that bitch picking through my cube?" he asked us, he *told* us. "One fine-looking lady!"

I'd seen better looking gas pumps, so I asked, "Spider, when was the last time you were tested?"

"Holmes, I'm serious," he said.

"We know you are," said my cellie.

"And we thought you had more heart than that," said Rolly.

Spider swayed in the aisle, only to look at Rolly and say, "Some of them are big in the Bible, too. The Bible says, 'Plentiful.'"

"Get off that shit," Rolly told him. "The Bible's nothing more than a law

Rock Salt & Glissandos

book."

"*I'll show you sass, you want sass, you hole eater?*" the ramp voice asked.

"But it's the *Bible*," Spider argued lamely.

Manther came up, a rolled cigarette smoking at his orange fingertips. His tattoos were clean, some of which he'd tacked on by himself. He sat next to my cellie, on my cellie's bunk, simply because he belonged. Rolly hit his Camel. I hit mine, my cellie hit his. Tombstone exhaled a large plume through the fly screen on his window, into the dust, into the sun. All the way from a reclining position on his bed. Manther was just there.

"Now, Juanita," I told Spider, "the one who did me, she had something to notice. Even though she ruined it by flaunting it to us like a torture."

"Yeah she did," said Manther. Always, he was direct.

"She didn't have *that* much," said Spider.

"What are you talking about?" Manther told him. "She was tight. I could see the wrinkle all the way from *my* crib."

Laughter. Beat the rest of the time down to hell.

"And when she got in here and started handling things, I nearly broke down praying from the agony," I said. "She set something off."

"OK," said Spider, "but I also noticed mine." He then turned and walked off, almost as if he were offended. The rest of us just hung around, blowing smoke.

"*You're just a sniveling little prick,*" came the ramp voice, "*sniveling!*"

"Got a problem? Huh? Got a problem?"

Manther held out his burned snub, glancing around the cube. I stood for an ashtray, looking again through my window. The earth was now gold, this high color that dust gets when it shimmers in the morning. The sky was blue and the sun was up there, continuing to explode over the run: you had to be able to disengage, I thought, for this really close-up sort of time. You only had to get over these walls. The trick was to walk away from your own fucking skeleton.

"Those books are stashed good, but if you want I can pick them up tomorrow," said Rolly.

"Whatever you think's best," I told him. "I'm with you."

"*Gonna cut off your pieces, motherfucker!*" said the ramp.

"*I'll show you a set you ain't never gonna get past!*"

I pulled out my writing board and sat it on top of a cardboard box. I put my ashtray down, and my cellie threw out a pack of smokes. We sat around the table waiting, listening; listening to the ramp voices and waiting on their sacked, venom lunch. Time, I thought, will never really get me.

The shakedown was over.

Steve Fisher

ball-peen thrush

    She's probably got something
right now

    this second

      going on

in her small twisting flesh—

    thin colored tubes
      of thought
      in her dome
      and a sprocket
of sensation near the rib heads.

    A vigor
    a dart
where the thighs meld out
      and a volt of hair
      as she sways
this direction and laughs.

You'll see a bell in her calf
    as her heel raises up
    and the toe weights the hold
as she swings it.

There's a wind in her head
    while something inside her
    over and over again
comes out—

    as her lips corner sparks
    and the husk of her syllables
enlarge the glass in her windows.

Rock Salt & Glissandos

There's a knob of fruit on her tongue

   there's
   a puckered
   merlot

       or
   a coil
   of Chablis
   raw,
       high-tonic
   buff

   and a sugar-pink-lungfire fur

   and an extra breath when she breathes.

   —Right now
       this second
           it's something
   rim-level and good.

Steve Fisher

dysphoria

You want to go forward.
To lunge with a great grin
of enthusiasm and sunlight.
You want to feel
   this
click-clack adrenaline,
this natural spirit of pace.
You want to tell someone how you feel.
You choose a common topic.

You tell them
and they feel different.
There's no law against
how either of you feel.
The law is very specific
   about
taking both sides.
Still, you have a problem:

someone always feels
that they're somehow
  right
about you:

"Listen," she says
"will you receive
transitional counseling
when you're released
from prison?"

Such wank.
As if you've forgotten
how to use a toaster,
   or fuck.
She's like an outback era

Rock Salt & Glissandos

and you're
   right here.

"I'll need fuck therapy,"
you tell her, "poignant
sex orientation."

It's the only response you have
and it's real.
She thinks it's a joke.

  It's also a joke.
  Yet it was her question.

Before sucking in the hemline
of this whipsong
you think:

  this mass-median
  dysphoria,
  how grossly it tempers
  our social code
  and times . . .

  You leave quickly
with the grin.
  A stadium of one.

Steve Fisher

boosted dream poem

I dream of her again,
wake up and lie still.
My eyes open.
Darkness.
Jesus, there's a funny
feeling in my chest.
The blood has stopped.
Cold.
My arms and legs function as
arms and legs—surprisingly—
and very faintly I
begin to see: lumps of shadows;
neon carcass formations.
Scabs.
But the arteries to my heart,
and the softness
circling my chest is solid.
Foundation block.
I don't know what to do.
Or, why she invades my REM.
Thoughts recede;
escape thru the blinds.
I press my arms
tight over my breastbone
and feel motion halt.

cactus fish

I woke up laughing.
It was morning, and the sky was a spread of grape juice mixed with orange pulp and the last of humming neon. I was on the second tier of the county jail with a sheet in a single cell, and the scabbed white walls soaked up the morning colors as if heaven, as spoken of, was really an option or existence. I lay on my pallet, softly laughing—thinking maybe I'll check out a razor this morning and shave. I'm obviously up early enough for that. And make the breakfast cart too . . . sell what I can't eat.
I got up and felt the blue concrete, cool on my feet, soothing my crumbling skin. Whatever had coupled me to, laughter was never far from my way of thinking, and as I came to, there was still a glow of previous sensation. I mockingly hummed a sort of brain-deafening jingle I'd heard the write-up guard, Fawl, whistle the night before. Fawl was one of these top-set and grievance types: over six feet and two hundred pounds of jailhouse law and order, a man without shadow or insight. He was Mexican, a Tucson Mexican, with a dark syrupy racial repugnance that dry-shimmered like a cropper in the field. His complexion reminded me of slightly burnt eggs, with these brown bubbling recesses that retained the oil. He was petty, he was loud, he was off-base with procedure and constantly hunting for inmate violations. When he took off his glasses, his eyes shone like a dirty toilet button. The kind of button the commodes in our cells were equipped with.
Why I was up so early wasn't something I was sure of. Like most people I went by the clock, but instead of the usual twenty-four hours I'd see twelve figures, multiply by three or four, then start assembling my day. Or cut the twelve figures in half or a quarter, which tended to prelude myself to belligerence—though primarily on the outside. I only guessed that a morning cycle had come around. But why the laughter? Well, why not. It was good

Steve Fisher

enough to react from completely within yourself.

The sky was now forming into a multi-colored animal marmalade. I stopped humming and splashed water on my face, then on my chest and armpits. It was almost 6:00, lock down would be over, and we'd be out of our cells for most of the morning. I let the water evaporate on my skin as the walls lightened up and the concrete turned gray.

The lights in the day room, which were always on, dimmed just a bit. A sharp, gnat-swatting sound like you'd hear from a smoke detector went off and, looking out the little window of my solid-cell door, I saw the morning guard, releasing the lower tier. Step by step, cell by cell, man by man. Tedium. This was about the only work he did all shift, since he came on when we were quarantined at 11:00, and left at 7:30. They were *supposed* to make room checks every half hour, but they mainly read magazines all night, talked on the phone, or cackled in a pud-lather with the roving sergeants and upper brassman who had rotated into the graveyard shift. Not that you wanted them peeking in your cell all night, but once in a while you'd need a match, an aspirin, or want a new magazine for yourself. Once or twice a year the paper would run a feature about all the stress the jailers were under. But it was never mentioned *why* they were unable to find alternative employment.

Stillbrook, the guard, wiggled his fat ass up the steps like a sixth grade teacher I once had, a red-headed woman with a huge lower face and gate-wide hips, who won all sorts of trophies as a stock car racer. We battled the whole year, but her advantage was she not only had the paddle, she had the principal and the assistant principal, and both were set against me. I'd win a certain amount of verbal battles, but if she was tired of losing she'd simply send me off to the high office, where they'd end up trying to expel me for a few days, usually over nothing. Toward the end of the year I was bored of it; heard of someone they called the district superintendent of schools, wrote him an honest letter about the abuse I was receiving from the teacher and her superiors, and—like that, in the words of the crooked parlance—she ceased and desisted hereunto. It was my first substantial victory as a para-lawyer, and as the Doors of Justice and their adjunct wings continued opening for me, I had a preparation that dated way back.

My cell opened and Stillbrook hollered "BREAKFAST IN TEN MINUTES," as if I was halfway down a city block from him, working a jackhammer into the street over a water main. I slowly put my jailhouse shirt on, tucking the collar wings and neckband under—homeboy-style—then buttoned up. There was a pot of coffee downstairs; I fixed two cups with creamer and sugar, took one up to my cell, sipped at the other, and came down with a cigarette going. Most of the guys didn't sleep very well in those concrete block rooms with the fluorescent nightstrip buzzing down on them; most, in fact, had bruises and cuts or other abrasions that the hard rubber palettes, or mattresses, deliberately aggravated and wouldn't absorb. They moved around the dayroom in a gimp and stutter, drinking the coffee, waiting for breakfast, and lining their

Rock Salt & Glissandos

pockets with packets of sugar and creamer... which they hid all over the pod.

The day room was about half the size of a basketball court, with a low count of chairs and plenty of bad air. I guessed that the germs of the first man who had entered that jail with a cold were still airborn. I grabbed a chair off the wall stack and sat down at a front table, smoking with a kid named Clem. A murmur and whine picked up as the coffee went down. Same old morning. Both TVs were on, tuned to the same cartoon show. They were in the rear, under the pillars. Which is why I was sitting up front. Our "pod" held thirty-six men. Of those who were up, at least fifteen were watching the sets. There were few other directions to look.

"Clem," I said to the kid, "you see that new one, leaning over by the set? With the string lip and the big eyes, on edge, kinda like he's waiting to be asked a question?"

"Don't like 'im," Clem said. "Looks like a guy who's gonna give evidence."

That's all Clem said about him as we finished our smokes. I wanted to ask if he knew of any apparent tension between this guy and a house-buddy of mine, a Yaqui Indian named Tony. But what I said to Clem was, "You're too quick to ever end up here again, but then they say that about me as well... got anyone on the outside to *disappoint?*"

"Nope," he said, "and I won't end up in here again, either. Somewhere else, maybe, but if I get out of Tucson fast enough, you'll never find me below altitudes of eight-thousand feet again."

For a twenty-year-old kid, that was some grand determination, I thought. One side of his face was heckled with zits. An orange patch had formed with the aid of the ointment the nurse was giving him, and you could see that the whole thing was going to dry up like that in a crust. It looked like certain parts of America I'd seen on relief maps. He lightly grazed over it with his index finger.

"Lord no," I agreed, as if I really understood what he meant about the eight thousand feet. But the only thing I knew was that he had a way out up there, and I didn't feel like going into the rest of it with him right then. Not only that, but impatience in jail was like getting a cannon ball right in the gut. You had to lay off, or go down. Simple as that.

But that was what it was all about, being involuntary members of this select social club: information was rationed in even smaller portions than the cooks were used to giving out, and what went uncomprehended at first was quickly placed within the tone of circumstance, lending a gravity to the abstract that pulled the point home—unless you were a total moron. It was simple scripture. Guys got into jams at times, just trying to *explain* themselves. Especially before a judge. You either picked it up or ended many ways from your own truth.

Clem, however, commented at his leisure. Maybe he knew of a special tier up there with all sorts of provisions, with large leafy plants full of oxygen and female guards who came directly from the pages of *Hustler*, full of all the

Steve Fisher

tricks, gratis. Every four hours a lazy Susan filled with powders, pills, pops and the works would be delivered by a non-uniformed volunteer with rubber soles on his shoes and a degree in something like Pro Tempore Inmate Pharmacology. They'd call this The Blue Oyster Pod, trim it out with wall-to-wall hazel carpeting, with just a little section of amber tile near the unlocked doorway and arrival desk. The rubber soles would be necessary to keep the noise level down, so the inmates wouldn't be disturbed when a volunteer entered. You'd do your time like a foodstamp millionaire living in the tropics . . . and the food? You bet. No gassed-up fruits or vegetables, the meat fresh from the local butcher, Bovine Joe; juices, bread . . . the whole schmere, ready for twenty-four hour vending. Any complaints would be handled quickly, with preferential discretion. It would be a period of time that began without shame and ended with a high-postured, silver exhilaration. But for now, at least, me, Clem and Tony were disgruntled members of the same murky, stocked pond, waiting on any number of bad, spring-loaded offers that our inept public defenders would recommend we accept.

The breakfast cart was wheeled into the sallyport, a small corridor of remote controlled doors, and a line quickly formed against one wall. Chairs were tipped into the tables as each inmate reserved a place to eat at. Then there was some cutting into line and the like, everyone starved for a foggy tray of gruel. Clem and I sat at our table, watching as the line jumped and passed by. Tony, who was up for every meal, stood calm and silently in the line, un-rushed, a waxy gleam in his eye that was almost un-noticeable. But somewhere in his head was a perceptible, disturbing thought. I could almost see it, wrapped up fiercely like a tight brussel sprout. Tony was also huge and bicepted all around, despite being addiction-trim.

"That chow line," said Clem with disgust. "Like they're trying to make the speed lane on the way into work. Just who the *hell's* in that much of a hurry to get to work?"

"Oh, the good guys," I joshed with him. "Isn't it always them? Might be cracked like a frayed end, but introductions all around before taking your sister out."

"I was working in a freezer in Juvie when that made a comeback, but I know my sister didn't get rich offa that trend."

Trend or not, some of these guys were in jail because they never bothered to ask the sister in the first place. One fellow even had this pitch as a carpet salesman: with a rolled-up carpet he'd knock on the girl's door, gain entrance, roll the carpet out and do her like that. Then he'd roll the thing up, maybe tie the girl down, and exit the building like an installation representative. I don't know what he told them at the booking desk when they asked his occupation, but the rotten thing he told the new arrivals — trying to establish himself — was that in fact he *was* an Installation Man. It was quickly decided that he either shut up or face the pod — many of whom had sisters themselves.

We picked our trays up after the line ran through and went back to our

Rock Salt & Glissandos

table. The oatmeal was cold, the powdered milk was warm, and the oven-baked luncheon meat was a disgusting, speckled pink thing that bowed up like a spitting tongue. And it had been fourteen hours since they last fed us.

But there were two items I could eat: a piece of steam-dampened toast (with grape jelly) and a small container of orange juice. I gnawed on the toast and wolfed the juice down; got a cigarette for the rest of my tray. Watched as most of the pod ate in ritual and languor. Some even ate the oatmeal—hadn't they paid credence to the rumors about that oatmeal?

Then I heard Spanish, rapid Spanish, just to my right. It was Tony, all of him, up and challenging the freak with the grass-blade lips. A blushing weight dropped through the pod as I watched the bulging eyes of Castello, the wetback target, fixate just slightly above and to the right of Tony. For all the glow on him under those house lights, he was as sightless and disoriented as a blind man in a cargo well. He was truly petrified.

The house watched, fascinated with Tony aggressing toward Castello. I didn't understand much Spanish but I did know *puto*, a word that Tony used repeatedly while going after the wetback, a word that means punk. I didn't know why he was flagging the *puto* down, but I did know that Tony was generally soft-spoken and somewhat interested in politics; a guy I played cards with while discussing a great world which we knew would never happen fast enough, if in the Bill of Odds at all. He was waiting on fifteen years, but from what I saw the fifteen would wait on him: his contentment seemed a natural thing, not a rubber approach. His attack had me more than curious.

It was simple enough, but years, it seemed, were flushed out in five seconds as Tony kicked a chair from his path. He landed an off-center punch to the guy's neck, just below his left ear. The wetback was big enough, full of brawn and bran, but again he seemed tunneled in shock and silence—as if the blow had produced a sub-physiology that might be construed while viewing a corpse. But as Stillbrook phoned for back-up, and the pod—like empty men in empty rooms who'd just alighted with the purest of revelations—rose hooting with sparks, Tony put a dead-bolt jab with the top of his knuckles into Castello's jaw, a dull fleshy crack seeping from his head as he went down. Two punches. Tony looked down, speaking slow Spanish before returning to his cell, words that Castello would later have to learn from the wetback minority.

Two things crossed my mind as I watched Tony walk up to his cell and close the door, waiting on the guards who would escort him to the isolation ward. One: no other fights broke out, so it was a matter of personal definition, not pod anxiety. Two: what they said about the quiet ones being effective fighters that you don't want to fuck with was not only true, but verified to those who thought it was a joke.

I headed up the steps with a coffee as Stillbrook dispelled the already roving inmates. Their chattering deflected off the walls, making the pod sound like a nest of newborn robins. Tony motioned me over through his window, in need of a smoke. "I'm out," I could barely hear him say through his cell. Then he signaled that he also needed matches. He'd discover, like all of us who went up there, a way to lace and smuggle them in, since cigarettes and fire were prohibited where he was going. So I only slipped five under his door, along with the matches. A pack would be way too obvious.

As he lit up, I tried asking what had happened, what it was all about. In scrambled words and gestures, as four jailers with cuffs and fetters formed a landscape at the C.O.'s desk, Tony told me how Castello had come from nowhere last night and started running his mouth off like a barking box and acting like an idiot. Tony let it pass then, but when Castello started this morning and refused to shut down, Tony altered into punches and the guy fell hard. "I felt like a can of Black Flag," Tony told me. "They oughta have a place for these smart-ass wetback punks."

"When you get up to Florence," I assured him, "you'll find that they do."

But that hardly mattered. Tony was getting pulled, while Castello would hang around until they had enough of his sort to transport back to Mexico. Then it would begin all over.

Five minutes later they had him secured, leading him down the steps while a female sergeant was actually *scolding* him for what had happened—"I WILL NOT TOLERATE fighting in MY jail," I heard her snap—without any real way of knowing what had actually occurred. Tony gave me the high sign while a guard was recklessly throwing his personal effects into his sheets. He then tied up the bundle and dropped it to the floor, like a slob. There was so much discouragement, so little warm water or soap or independence. We had twelve minutes left before the half-hour lockdown at 7:30, but Stillbrook now had a report to file. The sets were turned off, fast deals were made for smokes, and we were rushed to our cells as the foot-staff hustled dilemma, like a gas leak, on frantic edge.

It wasn't until noon or so that Fawl, the prowling write-up guard, buzzed into our pod to replace the regular man on duty. I was pacing my cell at the time, coffee and cigarette going, attempting to write a love poem to a short and seductive dark-haired woman who sweetened my dreams with mystical hillscapes and brushing flesh, yet always left me limp and dry. She'd lead me from one brilliant room to another in the great jeweled palace—a temple of dreams, a palace of exclusion—her dark foreign figure made and sought after only in fantasy and unknown countryside. From there she would lead me through humid botanical gardens and giant colorful trees, to riverbeds by the bog thickets, and lay herself out in full gown and body, which was crested with magnificent smelling hair that swam her face and shoulders. What does a woman such as this taste of, I'd think in the heat of those dreams? How do I unfold this girl, whose heart's so similar to mine, who only wants to be far from the assembled sentries? I'm not usually such a person, but this special reoccurring dream girl had ensnared me into making old-era provisions for

Rock Salt & Glissandos

the sake of blessed passion. And for that I needed elaborate spiritual access; a poem with a soulful headwind and staggering light that would one night reach her, declaring my love, thrashing the horsepaste from both of us. I'd have to be careful with this poem, bearing just right to compensate her, but I did have one thought if my approach returned failure: *she wouldn't be leaving me for a long time.*

I wasn't much of a poet. I had a legal pad and a couple of pencils, plus a felt-tip pen I had stolen from the old woman who pushed the library truck in once a week. I'd write a few love lines down, or whole stanzas of lust and adoration, but end up erasing the embarrassing, groaning grunts of lead. I wrote with pencil because I could save paper that way, and while I cleaned an eraser off with toilet paper, looking out my window, I noticed that Fawl had been in our pod for over forty-five minutes. I thought he was going to relieve the day guard, so's he could have a lunch break, but those breaks only last thirty minutes, time-locked as hell.

But that's how it sometimes worked: an incident, such as the one with Tony and the 'back, deliberated the shift coordinators into a stance. They'd send the regular guards from pod to pod, to durate a shift. Double them up. Shake us down for the sake of power and exhibit, often using the large, flubbery dyke-squad to do so. I can still see them slowly coming, hot-eyed and baby raper white, like a row of urinals mounted to a traveling wall. Piss-bucket commandos; newsprint stress victims: with all that stress, you'd think some would weigh less than two-hundred pounds — but they seldom appeared to.

So Fawl was going to be with us, a self-stated eight year veteran and son of a ranking officer, who had been forced to retire and quickly died. "Enforcement and sacrifice to his community was what he lived for. When he couldn't sacrifice his good intentions to the people no more, he died," I'd heard Fawl say to a group of goslings, as if referring to how God Himself, in His Golden Moments, once had really created *men*. Kuk-n-cud, I thought. But his ancestry aside, Fawl looked like a regular with the gout. Around forty, I'd say, with that frog-like pestiferous sheen that the electorate might rightly think cost the city an extra fifty alone in weekly uniform upkeep. He was not a hot burner, in my opinion . . . but being such an instinctual, rule-riding jail cop, perhaps someone at the news desk could circumflex this matter with carefully crafted editorial mediations.

I left my cell door just slightly ajar, resting it on the latch so I wouldn't be locked in. Most everyone was in the dayroom, either playing cards, watching the TVs or grouped at the tables, agreeing as to how they disliked this one or that one for one reason or another. Petty ostracism, really, as if they were the pod establishment making judgment calls on the ones they couldn't, for some reason, get a handle on and somehow influence. Barrel-bottom department heads, swathed in grifter's credentials, preparing for gladiator school. I'm sure my name came up a few times at first and they made their jokes, since I pretty much kept to my projects and myself, but when I was bored I'd go down and play cards with them or chat a bit, and soon my privacy was respected and I was just another guy doing time. I even passed along a good suggestion once in a while, like a consultant, which was appreciated. And of course I knew it was better to access myself in than to put up with any later shit. Always better to do this, in jail. Plus, I reasoned, there was always plenty of time, so I played with it . . . instead of sitting around a table while time knocked the emphasis out of me.

Fawl, at any rate, seemed busy. Besides slipping around the pod to utter his senior commandments, he carefully reviewed each inmate's file for new tickets, or write-ups. Which is standard procedure, except that Fawl's "dedication" bordered on a voracious type of intolerance, balanced by a retardant form of over-ethic which was unusually egotistical, even by jailhouse standards. The resulting scornful pettifog only dragged the pod down into the stinking fishweed, when part of the "pod concept" was to eliminate un-needed tension and altercations all around. It was a fair idea which cost almost nothing in discipline (a so-called *structure* being built-in to this approach), and it probably saved the city money—from court time to suspension pay— from lawsuits that would normally be filed by inmates in a wide open, lawless custodial environment. But Fawl was one of the few exceptions; a cop with no need for the briefing room with his heritage and his leadpipe attitude, deranged into the role of a sort of Third Reich Den Mother, AmeriMex-style. Just three days earlier he had searched my room for violations, finally writing me up for supposedly having an over ration of creamer packets. Nobody else really gave a damn, but Fawl gave me the twelve-hour lockdown for a first-time offense. (The creamer is indeed so non-dairy that it ignites like flashpaper, so the idea behind rationing it out is that with our inherent "criminal" status we'll all hoard and amass the stuff, make pipe bombs out of toilet paper tubes and blow our way out of the place from eight stories up—even if we're just catching up on a hundred dollar traffic fine, payable at ten dollars a day.)

The 2:30 headcount came quickly for me. My poetry may have stunk, but I found a sort of upper-existence in the process of writing it that ripped the latches and hardware completely out of my mind. I think it worked up a metabolism that made the coffee bleed through my system like amphetamine, too, but without that trembling residual come-off I've heard about. I only roared on in my cell, writing a poem that wouldn't be going to any publisher. But of course I had an idea of submission: hers.

I hardly noticed when Fawl KICKED my door shut for the count. And then I did, becoming aware of the relative silence in the place. They were changing shifts at this time, which meant a thirty-minute lockdown was in effect. I dropped to the floor and did twenty-five push ups as the long rectangular sunlight circled my room and burned against the walls. I washed my hands and splashed myself with water, then sat on the bed and stared.

A pall tightened my cell as Fawl entered with the new shift—a young, almost pre-twenties blond named Ginger who was built with a figure that could probably have gotten her a cheerleading scholarship to a dozen different colleges. But she was a cop, for some reason, and her flesh was completely oriented to that pale brown uniform. Tight, I mean, and almost sensually menacing—a fact she was well aware of. I never asked why she was a cop, but she had this shrug and aloofness about her that made me think the inside of her head must be entirely bleached out. Some day she'd be a street cop— that was her goal—and probably get married to a phys-ed teacher from a local high school . . . or maybe a higher-up, such as a football coach. But now she was with Fawl, backing the cretin up while everyone was placed in static, working with him and his plan against me.

"What is it?" I asked Fawl. He was leafing through a stack of papers in the corner.

"Check his bed out," he said to Ginger.

She just looked at me and I stood up, moving out of her way. I was thinking the obvious right into her eyes, but saying it would get me another two to five years for "sexual harassment." I smiled.

Ginger folded the mattress up, found nothing, then opened it and ripped off the sheets. It wasn't there. Fawl began rummaging through my desk.

Two weeks earlier I had eaten a pork chop that was so stiff and old it was more like eating a clothespin than meat. Spears of gristle had lodged between my teeth, and I tongued one out as Fawl came up with the evidence. A rotten taste swelled through my mouth, and I spit the thing against Fawl while his back was still turned. Then I noticed Clem and a few others, watching from their windows.

"This is BIG time," Fawl said, holding up the felt-tip pen. "Even I didn't expect to find this."

Probable cause was not needed to search someone in jail . . . elsewhere too, I hear.

"It's only a pen," I said. "Why don't you keep looking until you find something that makes more sense?"

Fawl flicked the little pocket clip on the pen as Ginger moved to my side. I could only try acting naive until an explanation was given, but I knew why my pen was outlawed: the metal clip could be removed and filed down a bit, so you could use it as a key to unlock certain types of handcuffs. If you could pass through the metal detectors, and un-cuff in a Sheriff's van on your way to court, say, then you'd only need about twelve sets of miracles to ensure your escape, freeing yourself from everything but the books and records and investigators.

"You're on investigative lockdown starting now," he said, delighted with himself. I knew that was coming, but a strange moaning silence still figured in my ears.

"On what charge, huh? What's the call in this matter?"

"This is contraband. You'll get my report in a while."

"That's a pen. Now why don't you clearly state the charge, instead of playing kindergarten, and we'll get on with it."

"I've stated the charge," he said. "Now it's up to the hearing officer to decide on the matter."

"But there's no implication to your statement, Fawl; you're not saying a damn thing. Now are you going to substantiate the charge verbally, as you're required to, or are the words lodged in that greasy gullet of yours?"

He seemed to foam in the head for a moment, as if a physical sense or disgust for me had overcome him. Equals? Ginger said nothing, unless you happened to be looking at her hips.

Rattling. Fawl said, "Possession of contraband and insubordination to an officer. That remark of insubordination will get you forty-five days of separate isolated confinement."

"Ginger," I said to her, "maybe you can explain the difference between a functionary of the jail system to him, and that of being a simple inmate. You know as well as I do that I would have to be a paid member in the chain-of-command here to be guilty of insubordination — right?"

She hesitated a moment, the dilemma of an issue being upon her. Everyone who had passed through the jail while I was there had wanted to fuck her, including me, but I didn't gloat on the yard over it like some of them did. One inmate, a fellow named Chester, once told me—"She looks better than a bitch I once done named Roxanne, and she was *hot*," between pumps on the Universal machine. "Yeah," I told him, "and by the way I'm feeling, I'd lay you odds she could bring me off by hand." That was all we needed to say about her, but it triggered a friendly partnership between us. We shared our tobacco and so forth until Chester quietly disappeared in the D.O.C. van one morning, gone like the thinnest decay of plucked harpsichord wire.

As Ginger weighed the thought, I remarked a little encroachment to Fawl:

"You know, preceding jail house policy in a matter requiring due process will get you an appointment with *your* superior, Major Donaldson. You can allege whatever you want, but of course I'll be submitting paperwork of my own . . . interviewed as well. I imagine, since he likes to consider himself the power-arm of this joint. Especially when it comes to protocol."

Ginger cleared her throat, signaling to Fawl that I could have a point . . . and maybe it would be best to back off a little. Then she decided to Fawl that "I think we have enough to handle this matter ourselves, don't you think? Possession of contraband, in his case, is a serious infraction and I think we should write it up as such."

Fawl's eyes seemed to stiffen into the frames of his glasses, as if they had suddenly grown to the size of human ears. He thought he had really nailed me on that last charge, but now he only had a brittle temper, magnified in the large square lenses of his glasses, like wax.

"You're a real smart ass, and I don't like smart asses a bit," he let me know. "Your problem is that you have an attitude problem, but I'm gonna give you a break and just charge you with contraband. You're lucky as hell I don't push the other one."

He scanned my cell for apparitions, it seemed, then glanced at Ginger. "We're finished here," he said. "Lock him down and prepare to move him."

"All right," Ginger told me, "roll up. I'll be back in a while to move you. Don't forget to separate your contraband."

"Move me where?" I was all settled in.

"I'll have to find out. Just start separating your smokes and your . . ."

"This is all a bunch of shit—don't you agree?"

"It's possible," she said with a fringe of sympathy in her voice, "but I have to follow his orders. He's been here longer than me. He's been here almost a year."

I was startled. Nobody had checked him out. They were all copping pleas paper blind. All those years of loyalty and tradition, of jail house dedication and senior eligibility he spoke of—where were they?

"WHAT?" I asked her.

"He's been working here for about eleven months," she explained, "and I'm pretty new, so I have to follow his directives."

"You're positive? Then where was he before he started working here?"

"I'm not exactly sure, but I think he was managing a 7-11 down around Nogales somewhere. I'll be back in a while."

"I guess you know about the people you work with?" I asked her.

"Most of them," she said, "yeah."

Her body weaved slowly as she left my cell, lisping at the sunlight, and thick, as if she was pushing against something besides the stagnant air. It reminded me of scuba divers I'd seen on film, flipping through that murky liquid slop—so beautiful—around the coral tendrils. Before she closed my door I noticed a pair of Reeboks on her feet. *She* was in violation there, for the uniform code specified that all guards wear these gourd-stomping leather boots, which laced up to the shin. I noted it with the thought that I might have to use it against her, or bargain, perhaps, for a favor.

Well shit, I was thinking about Fawl, here's a pitiful shelf inspector from a convenience market in the sun-dark region of lower Arizona, a place of toddling cacti and desert shrub, flowered into the tough, dry, sub-earthly dust, passing himself as a long standing jail house authority. I know at times that truth is crossed as a diffuse matter of judgment, similar to a ballpark umpire (and especially true in a court of law), yet it's also a towline between grief and peddler, between pride and abnegation, and the truth that wins out isn't always a correct identification—as in Fawl's case, which itself was emerging to me now. Arrogance I could tolerate, since there is usually a tone of realism and flame involved, but arrogance, combined with his self-infatuation, his lies of leadership and great predecessors, amounted to nothing more than a chain of smock and pretension. And it was not a form of mental ataxia; it was a mangled blubber of competitive authority; fornix assumed to be under control.

(And to borrow from Algren):

For here was a man of slick rhubarb skin, oiled in swart macho dreams of misconduct and self-fornication; of extensive mis-scripture to the life of the just; a phantom to his shadow as he moves through the longest rays of the lowered slanting sun.

(Continued):

A man of iron and concrete enclosures from crib to cranium to workday; a Mexican, a cadet, foothold to a clinch of reality where lies are not nightmares, but a gift to survival. A man new to the cons, but not the con—a Cactus Fish, as it were—cactus formed into Mexican; fish supplied to the unacquainted and newly disoriented of the *works*.

That was how I regarded him—Cactus Fish—now as I rolled up for transfer. Ginger had brought me the traditional plastic garbage bag, and into it went my sheets, my toothbrush and paste, a load of legal and other papers; state-issued pants and shirts, my pencils and poetry . . . along with twenty or so matches, ripped from the book and tucked under the head grips of two legal pads, with a striker I also divided. It was more sensible to separate these items, because when the shakedown came and if they were discovered in one pad, the assumption (and oversight) was they had netted your booty and foiled a smuggling attempt.

I had about three items of no-no's: seven packs of cigarettes, still in the carton, and two candy bars. I could care less about the candy, but the cigarettes were another matter: I smoked like an insane armless bastard with a Camel taped to his lips. Five smokeless days in isolation might somehow fortify my body, but I was in no mood for earning points . . . be them from heaven or cell biology. So I left a pair of pants on the wall prong as a sort of overlooked item, slipping four packs of Camel's into the pockets. Through my study of in-house shakedowns, clothing, on the wall for some reason, was rarely inspected. And since they'd rip apart my trash bag before "placing" me elsewhere, the odds leaped in their favor of my smokes dropping down into sight. But this way I could dump the stuff out, sort through it, then coolly say something like, "Oh shit, best not to forget my pants"—or whatever spontaneity would be necessary.

The plan worked. Fawl was gone, everyone was out, and Ginger did the shakedown in haste. If I didn't get transferred to another pod (where I'd be shaken once more), I'd be in business.

I didn't move far, but the new cell was horrible. It was zoned within twenty feet of the C.O.'s desk, but worse, right next to the "suicide watch" cell. A suicide watch can reason-out easily to understanding, but the thing about it is that they patrol the suicidal every fifteen minutes, logging the entry book with short accounts, describing the guy's behavior. Most don't have any, if you've ever noticed . . . and I don't just mean in jail. But as long as they were checking into 3B-1, chances were that they'd lean over to 3B-2, my cell, just to grin in passing the idea of how fucked it was supposed to be when you're unable to mingle, scam, use the phone or play cards with your fellow ilk. It never occurred to them this might be a holiday, of sorts, for me. My worry was that I might be caught smoking and sent to the hall of maniacs for forty-five days, just as they had done with Tony.

However, my broad acquired knowledge did the intrinsical alertness for me, something I learned from watching a young kid who'd been given the same five days as me about two weeks before. The nance would light up and smoke in the center of his cell, with a column of sun just stationed on his Bugler, or whatever he smoked, but at any rate exposing his "offense." They escorted him off within fourteen hours, the ass, because his nicotine hunger just ossified his lameness.

But with a bit of precaution, my way was almost foolproof: you're on the edge of your bed, next to the wall, with an ashtray obscured by your papers or trashcan. You check on the guard, light up, then cheek the white walls and exhale up high. The smoke has disappeared in the wall without fog or bellow, then the butt is flushed with the ashes and you're almost home free. The final measure is to flap your mildewed towel like a *capote*, snapping the smell of that molecular tobacco into the reeking stench of that tight and diseased oxygen, something like an atomizing, rancid, wind-thrust of a flag.

So I had my smokes and a bit of solitude, but even that solitude was sorta like living in your local city backweed camp. Even though the cell door was two inches of steel, the TVs blared like some fringe-freak gone mad . . . decrepit, with ever increasing GAIN, or volume. Another problem was the chow line — a procession of hooting felons, with the shortest of steps, parading past my window. It wasn't their fault that the line traveled like a worm — I wasn't pissed at them — it was all in the slow delivery of the trays by the guards — a matter of instruction and training; of graduate work, no less — to make sure no one got more than an un-ample meal. I knew it, they knew it, so I just lay on my cot, waiting for the last cold tray. Even that could take an hour. At better times a smoke, some sugar, or a magazine was slipped under my door by one of the population . . . and a fellow risking this, if nabbed by a guard, was himself exposed to being locked down. Naturally, this is why we had all sorts of codes and methods. And of course, this was why certain guys were left the hard way. Jail is not a place of particular worship or lasting bond, but it is an almost exclusive development, designed and rigged-out for the advancement of what the house shrinks and their kind might erroneously term, yet absolutely believe, as "self-regenerating incompetents." You might want to remember that on the highway at three a.m., with only one tail light burning. Or say you're jaywalking, with a prior DUI conviction . . . or hanging around a construction site, after hours, for any reason at all: that's my advice to the headstumps and gregarious types who aren't familiar with the practice of "interviewing a suspect's jacket." You may think you're in the clear from that sniveling little road infraction years ago, but once inside a prison or jail, or even on the streets, it's incredibly easy to find yourself a hundred branches from the fall.

Aside from the proliferation and noise, along with the concrete tremors one felt on the first tier, I managed to turn my time into a seasonal crest of sorts, a time within time, a body coming to juncture. I had sent letters around the world and went months without music or flesh; now I would have to prepare against Fawl, Ginger, and the tittering slide of the disciplinary committee — which consisted of nothing more than a deficient female orderly (about the lowest on the pole except for pumping gas into the judge's cars), who had a dull linoleum glaze in her eyes and a Xeroxed form to which you replied against your charge by checking either the "guilty" or "not guilty" box, though it hardly made a difference when the final reality of the tune was handed down. Staff promotions are simply not passed along to the objective jailer, especially one that functions as a minion's voucher. Her only role was to validate the existing citation, then formalize her opinion of your "attitude" on a prepared graph. Even that was made easy for her: one box read "acceptable attitude," the other, "bad." Since she wasn't exactly schooled in discretion, my guess was the only criteria needed was an ability to recognize how *she* felt at the time . . . then check off the box, capacitating her duty. The sham, as it were, was wired like a schematic throughout the jail.

Since she was so marginal, it didn't matter to me what she was going to do. I was already in confinement, and had other plans for Fawl — the sort of things you did without forms or procedures. I lit another smoke and wondered if Ginger's head really was made of chalk bone, then catnapped through a quick nightmare of diesel engines and powder puffs.

At some point the next day I started demanding a legal call. It takes almost longer than forever to get these bastards moving, so I kept up the noise between lines of poetry to the girl in my dreams. I wondered if she ever slept, but decided not to write it down; to just hand it over to her like that. I thought of a few other things, about her, about me, about faulty ventilation and the legal system. But I got my call that afternoon during lockdown — unbelievably — and my lawyer was actually there. After he agreed to meet me around two thirty the following afternoon, and with my head propelling in undercurrent, I thought about why vengeance was now an essential way of existence for me. Friction caused only by Fawl's slimy aggression and tricked-out foremanship threw scenes of my trips to Boothill in focus and blended with the notion of how stripped down my life had become. But instead of getting restless and ankle tight in the ugly available distracting options, I worked right off the skeleton, through a dozen grisly hemispheres of foghorn, rift and pallor. My joke was that it was sort of an inverted inspiration; a deaf laugh rally because the illusion was that you went by the rules — that cut-dated vocabulary which got you nowhere — to simply live — with nothing while being thankful it got no worse than that. I enjoyed going along with it to a certain degree, like special tribes scattered across the globe . . . but the staff relied on it, in the deafest of ways. They thought they had you, nut for nut, move for move, concrete to shackles. A blueprint, a kidney punch to the conscience and spirit. I only figured my mobility was limited, not my headscape or freedom of discretion.

The other reason I needed to anchor myself against Fawl was because once they got on you, it became the dross repetitive landscape of centuries, of oppressive brace and rural roads to a gray dawn of continuous, bleeding heartsap. You've heard of the pattern, no doubt. My way out of this was to have a turret gun mounted in my head. It was the same principal as Clem's eight thousand feet—only I didn't need the signing of release papers to get there. Only access to my lawyer which, by law, they couldn't deny me. I couldn't leave the system itself, but, within my thoughts, time fluttered like a wren in a berry bush . . . meadowlarks now and again sprang through my head, with warm, transient, dabs of tonal hue and tint, undemanding—or pounding that long center nail through my quick organ. But living on so many pallid edges, the perfect companionship in jail was entropy, in dissolving frames of time that bring the God in and then let Him go along in other directions. But I've felt that same way for as long as I can remember. For me, it was a constant.

They got the word, fiddled with their walkie-talkies around two o'clock that day—my third of isolation—and began making calls. Yes, my lawyer was there, so I was ushered to the elevator. The doors closed, and I waited like a fly in a shoebox until they decided to run me down. As a diversional snash, I waited about twenty minutes. Determination always screwed up control of their manual, so to speak, and I hunkered down, greased from scalp to pores and follicles in house sweat, waiting for the thing to drop. An outlook, a feeling circulated through my body like a swelling medicinal lather, an inward sponge bath of sorts, paradoxical and completely false to my outward scruff and stench. But, ironically, I gleamed like a freshly waxed and buffed corridor. When I got off the elevator, Fredrick, the hall cop, recognized me right off. Showered and scrubbed, he might have had to consult his log to figure out who I was.

"I see you've been showering with the toilet brush again," he said, leading into that escort conversation. "Ask for some water next time, if you ever straighten up."

Fredrick was all right because he accepted the polarity between us—not a hardass at all—and he liked joking as he led us to wherever it was we were going. His laughter, though soft and facially quirked with a barber's satisfied expression, came from an intimate delight of knowing that most of us were on our way to prison . . . something that charmed him, but he rarely spoke of it.

Wanting to catch the boys coming out of the briefing room for the new shift, I walked slowly with him and fed into his joke.

"Fredrick, you oughta know that I'm working in the kitchen now. Kitchen

Steve Fisher

detail, that's what you're whiffing. In fact, I just got off shift to see my attorney. How's your appetite?"

He skipped over that remark.

"That so?" he said, not pounding at the fact that I was coming from the third floor.

"Sure it's so, believe you me. Hard work, too, but tonight—tonight it's Salisbury steak, gravy, diced carrots with half-pats of margarine, and bread pudding for desert. Nothing short of memorial."

"You boys always did have it good in here, yes sir."

"Understand that you boys usually join us—in separate quarters, of course." A wind duct from overhead blew my order from behind us into the air we were stepping into. "You'll be wanting seconds, maybe thirds tonight."

"I think I'll be wanting a very quick temporary transfer if I see the commander coming out of the briefing room with the other boys 'bout now," he said, pretending to be offended.

Then he grinned. This guy *had* been around for years, so long that his belly resembled an ordinary sofa cushion, and his soft, white face, although backroad red, appeared riddled with masonry deckling. We came to a check point, a place where the three o'clock shift was milling around before heading off to their pods. Thirty officers would be a rough guess; tan uniforms, blemished, young and mostly big. As they laughed, I flashed on a lodge meeting of some kind that my grandfather had taken me to when I was a boy of about four or five. Nothing before me was short of that freak show way back when, I thought, knowing that my lawyer was locked only a few wings away under completely different conditions, near the security check-in post. We all waited on something here, but the major difference I noticed—downstairs—was how much money was being made while doing so. My ravaged presence—even with a public defender—could probably cover a hunk of mortgage or car payment for him, which was fine by me, yet also absurd when you stood it up like a post and considered the "logic" behind freedom through money, while the judge sat gravely in his chambers with reams and reams of law books and whatever vice suited him, grooved and wrinkled into his lips. Aside from the judge, though, I could easily imagine my lawyer using this conference money to buy him a weekend fiasco with a woman of some sorts, some young doxy his wife knew nothing about. My muted heart laughed around it all, because I intended to make money at some point myself—legitimately, of course. What would be the options when I got out— besides wine, women, song and doctors? Well, there was always a little place you had to rent, for starters, something I was never very good at holding on to, but I quickly dropped it: bigger things not only were in mind, but right in front of me.

"One for attorney visit," Fredrick told an eight-buck-an-hour form handler. The guy took my card and began filling the paperwork out. Then I saw Gratiot, a guard I knew and counted on, to come on duty.

Rock Salt & Glissandos

"Gratiot, my buddy," I told him, "hear about Fawl?" I started easily. He was black, young but slightly older than the rest, laughing it up with about a dozen of his colleagues. He looked up at me — down, actually — with this concurring facility beaming on his face.

"Sure I been hearing. 'Bout what?"

"Fast fraud," I said. "He's been lying. Not only to us, but to you guys as well."

"Hold on there a second," Gratiot said slowly, stepping forward. His friends cooled down, checking this out as he showed interest in me. A small audience gathered behind him, leery of me. I repeated myself so they all heard it correctly.

"Denny *Fawl*, man; you're talking about Denny Fawl?" he asked.

"Yeh. There's a few things about him you might want to be aware of, especially if he's ever tried to out-rank you."

I was the size of a pool cue compared to Gratiot, a guy who looked like he went through twenty-dollars worth of groceries a day and worked out as well. My advantage, under these circumstances, was that he probably figured I wouldn't lie to him. Which was true, so he remained there like a trail head.

"All right baby," he said, "I'm listening."

He and about fifteen others: a good starting point for creating dissension among the ranks. I was on. A bit feather nerved, but I didn't waiver.

"Well, we could start with his simple inconsistencies, involving — *affecting* — other members of your staff. Fawl's placed me in isolation at the moment, over a pen he found in my desk — same pen Jones and Kirkland here (I pointed) have used to fill out their papers when they were in my room. No problem, right? But when I mention to Fawl that other officers have used the thing, he starts blaming YOU guys for not doing your job . . . like you don't know shit from shine, or how to handle this with proper discretion. He implied that your conduct was so lame that you were all chicken shit when it came to enforcement."

"Fawl said *that*?" he asked, waiting for more.

"In words, somewhat marginally," I said, "but the implication was certainly there. Yet in his actions and attitude, that's exactly what he said. And, as we all know, a man's attitude in jail *is* his voice, whether or not he's a con or a cop — agreed?"

Gratiot sent a signal to one of his own, and the guy walked off just like he knew where he was going. It could be good news for me, I thought. Already, the dogs were tracking.

"Sure I agree," said Gratiot. "Attitude is the key basis for order around here, right?" Some of the cops shook their heads in agreement and made small comments. Gratiot wheezed out a somewhat serious laugh, straightened his belt buckle to be in line with his fly, then placed his hands on his hips in that take-charge manner cops do, as if it was some form of cult religious practice, usually with a pedestrian sacrament trapped on the side. And in an obtuse sort of way I suppose it was, but really it was just another academy psych-job, believing it helped their officers to dominate, through stance and expression. It brought to mind profiles of cadaver dogs I'd seen and read about, these "innovative and ferocious-faced beasts that certain sheriff departments were growing fond of."

"But a pen ain't so much as to make him bad jowl us," Gratiot continued, "least it shouldn't be."

"Yeah," another cop said, "it don't quite sound right, 'less you're messing around yourself. That it?"

I just looked at him like he was some sort of posthole dug by a work crew. His hair gleamed with dip, and I felt like asking if he blew his nose upside-down. But of course I had to let it pass.

"What else you got to tell me?" Gratiot asked patiently.

"'Malfeasance,' I believe the Major would call it, but judge for yourself. He's been telling our entire pod that he's an eight-year veteran, that he has total seniority and jurisdiction to override any rule in the code book, and it's simply not true. And from what I understand, he's only been here about a year."

Fredrick was about ready with my paperwork. I could see him squaring it away.

"No single officer has the authority to invent the rules as he goes along, if that's what you're telling us," Gratiot informed me, rolling his head from side to side to benefit the others, "and if he is misforming his work record, I'd have to agree with you that the captain would probably have a strong opinion about it and investigate the matter."

"And maybe not stop with Fawl's ass either, "I suggested.

"But it could be a term of malcontent within the ranks if he's right, couldn't it Sarge?" another asked Gratiot.

"It could be a wild party for the press, if they sent the right reporter over," I said as if I believed it.

"Look," said Gratiot, stepping close to me and talking in a flat buddy tone, "what is it you want? Let's get to it."

"Like the officer said, I hate seeing discontent among the ranks, specially when it affects me."

"And?"

"Think of it yourself; if he's got me singled out to earn points, to make his mark through deceit and petty-ass covert swindles which probably won't be reviewed, consider that he may have a select entry log on you and your partners that he'll one day submit anonymously to the captain. It'd be an uproar no matter what. You know, he *thinks* he's a sort of as-yet-to-be-erected statue, a bronzed hero on horseback . . . pretty obvious he's on another level, though. I'd say it's a kind of battlewig endurance psycho-stupor, and if I had your connections and respect around here, I'd marshal out the facts before he shows up at midnight with a headful of crickets—bi*polar* crickets at that!—

Rock Salt & Glissandos

capable of just about anything."

"Man," he laughed, "you're like a carnival act the way you talk—"

"Yeah, but it's all a form of money or favors . . . "

"—but you've also got this serious nature blended right into you which makes sense to me, so I'm gonna do some checking on Fawl for you—"

"*And* for yourself, Gratiot. What kind of an audience would I have if your men were suddenly floorwalkers at the nearby Osco?"

"—and see what this leads to."

"I can guess what it leads to: a decrepit vengeance coupled with an incompatible geriatric swell. He could go off at any moment, screaming the sweating tremors like some sort of human molotov if he's challenged in a no-win, no-way-out situation. He's an arrogant bastard. I'll bet he thinks his balls are as heavy as a mailman's pouch."

"Yeah, but I'm still the one who's trusting you. Now what's that make me?"

"A man with a talent for scouting the future?" I looked over. "Well shit, Fredrick's coming any minute now."

"OK, what do you want, and make it quick. Can't promise a thing though; you know that."

"Naturally. But I want smokes, and a room on the second tier away from the televisions. I want to rejoin the population and that's it."

"I'll see what I can do. And remember, be RIGHT with me."

"I gave you right. You'll be surprised at how much wrong you dig up with it."

Gratiot and the boys with the smiles and the emblems just seemed to nudge each other and swirl off like a buzzing floormat, some waiting on the "attitude" cases, others merely swagging along like wet mops in a dry gulch. Up in Phoenix our elected were deep in conference, mystified as to whether our consumers should be taxed another penny in the check out lines . . .

Fredrick moved up with my forms and his corridor keys in hand. As he unlocked a door he said, quite accurately, "You know the way," and I walked down the inmate's side of the visitor's row, back to where another locked door buzzed, leading to the attorney cubicles. That inmate's row, with its maximum seals and bullet-proof glass enclosure, reeking so bad that it pricked my nose like some sort of placenta fungus with cleats. My eyes watered in the salt of this collective sweat as if I was in a pucelage quarry, and when I rubbed a socket with my pinky, a distasteful pulp drained from my nostrils, down into my throat, and settled atop my ulcer. I hacked it out between video monitors , braced with new strength as my lawyer greeted me with an easy smile, just as if we were sitting down to a round of drinks and a steak.

"What's going on," he asked me, leaning back in the stiff chair, his suit coat spreading open. The cigar-brown tie he wore fell down his shirt and chest just right, like a manager working retail. But he didn't have that braggart's ego and slick windshield shine associated with the retail-types I had once worked for, until I couldn't tolerate the boss or the place any longer. But that was no issue now, hardly a garden of knock-weed and confusion, and I sat as calmly as he did, smiling, folding my arms across the tiny work table, just as if I was ready. I was, and I liked Tommy just fine. It was always good to see him, a guy on my side offering more than routine trade-offs. I explained to him what had happened with Fawl, and how just by showing up we may have accomplished an internal twist in my favor, "and really, that's about all I wanted to see you for today. Besides your good company, of course," I told him.

He understood right off, having spent years listening to his client's describing jail house conditions. He'd get a rock or two off, from something like this, but he also questioned the score without hesitation.

"I can only wait and see if I took him out," I said. "Just a little flair of time, that's all there is to it."

"We both know that it rarely happens," he told me, "and there's always retribution to consider." He relaxed even more, cupping his hands behind his head.

"Like I said, the beauty of this should be as a result of the other cops putting their breath on him. That's what I had in mind. That's what the idea was all about. You think the captain would do anything about it? Fawl's status, if you will, has been thrown into circulation with the right people. It'll get looked into, Tommy: I know the bullwhip logic these guys use, just as you do. And it would seem that they aren't going to let one moron centralize their ranks. The risk to them is an increment of exposure which could lead to any number of premature judgments and inconclusive finalities. Would you want that on *your* shoulders?"

The point being made, Tommy cracked his lips up and we dropped the matter, setting it aside for knock-around talk. We hit briefly on my case—a fifth-class felony with a prior conviction—touching on strategies to have the prior dropped, which could reduce my time by three to five years. I had come from the prison to clear up this matter and would be going back, but it really wasn't even a point of discussion that afternoon: my trial was a lax month away, the immediate was where time and possible troubles were gagging up. But now that Tommy had done his bit by showing at shift change, he motioned the guard to call down his next case. We must have spent a total of twenty minutes together, but I felt like I had just gone on a spree. While the guard cleared my paperwork we set another date for pre-sentence discussions, loafed for a moment, shook hands while I took a look at the sun outside, then I was on my way back up with Fredrick slowly behind me as we moved toward the elevator. Passing through the visitor's block I thought of all the songs heaven and defeat could hold, of those songs and pleas that went through the phone cords to the granite lungs of women and parents who had absolutely nothing in terms of movement to offer their scalding

Rock Salt & Glissandos

ones on the other side of the glass, then I was up in my pod, back in the isolation cell. But while I could still see a clock I noted it was only 3:15. Gratiot and the rest of the new shift were just getting into their pods and log books, and with any luck at least ten others were doing the same, all with Fawl on their minds. Jail, I was thinking: just enough tension, salt-lick, desperation and open wounds for the seemingly arbitrary to become mandatory, at least mandatory enough so's to widen my girth against Fawl's. I stretched on my bed and thumbed an old copy of *Popular Mechanics*, listening to the cotton-like mull of voices, TV, chairs, horns . . . *whiners*, reverberate my door. It was close to chow time, but I was thinking of Ginger and imagining, imagining . . . then I tried following an article on how to construct your own thermal windows. The instructions dizzied me and I started at the ceiling, my eyes rolling as if I'd been given the chloroform and sodium pentathol just prior to surgery. But on top of that I had a thermal window, an inescapable two-inch strip which ran nine feet up the wall. The article only wanted to keep the rain out, so all I had was another useless magazine. I closed my eyes and simply drifted away from my central axis, a depraved—but momentary—inertia running through me something like the "Gosling" passage, a short bit of music I couldn't name from an otherwise alright bit of symphony. I was dripping with a perfect glaze of porcelain sweat—still hacking up the custard from downstairs—growling it into the waste basket just to my right. But I was so used to these physical contortions by now that it truly seemed like second nature to me; it *was* an expected condition, almost and for all of us: shortly after the "five-minute flu," as I called it, a smile returned to my way as I remembered Gratiot, and I sat up on my bed, thinking of this as a valid extension—an inner-tech person, as it were, gone through thirty counter-clockwise headspins without losing balance at the edge of it all, or dwindling into a sloven reality. All my appetites—from lust and poetry to fitness and food were stations of flame—bargains, now that my control had returned . . . and all I had to do was milk time again, not duel with it, since it could easily break me into Psalms of discoordinated machete cartilage. I weaved in and out of this thought of time, considering it rubber rimmed in mason jars, tucked far away in a dark geography. A place I might be headed for. Was probably headed for, for no justifiable reason. A dangerous place, especially if you thought about it while bone weary and pitch frail . . .

But I wasn't under any illusion when this thin guard with a high finch-like voice opened my door—my cell—and instructed me to roll up, because I'd been transferred back to my old cell. "Take your time," he said off the rear of his tongue. "The other fellow is still cleaning up in there."

It was Gratiot, it was broadcasting just right, it was the thing working out.
"Sure, " I said, "what about chow?"
"We're keeping a tray warm for you," he said. "Saving some butter, too."
"Reasonable of you. I'll get this mess together before the butter melts."
As he waddled off, really looking like a lame pooch, the resolving note, or

cadence, came at once to me like a tortious fly: I could feel the computer checks on Fawl by Gratiot (and whatever else he looked into), and the impact it was now having on me (and him); I was flying; he was calm and determined in his own style, and I was at the gate, so to speak, waiting for the payoff at the wire. I was on my way.

So I was rolling up, and a fellow came by with cigarettes and ashtray as a type of salute. Always these smokes, I thought, as I lit up like a respected inmate again. I noticed though, that wherever the tray was, it didn't matter. Smoke was simply attracted to flesh. At another interval I *might* be curious about this form of thermal dynamics, but the belt had loosened from my head and I was ready for the next step: my old room, the phone, the yard, card games, legal consultation for food trays; stamps, envelopes . . . and spinal attachments, on and on. You could easily say I was in a state of staccato, but fiber laced, not rat framed. I did, however, honk up a deepwad of phlegm in celebration. It sounded like a cheap opera as I flushed it down the stainless.

Gratiot moved when he had his suspicions, but even though it brought a form of trust not usually shared between Them and Us, it was going through the motions, which all final steps take in jail—a type of censored nirvana would slowly evoke the deal and it wouldn't mean much down the line—it was just a trust we both benefited from at this point in time—and from now on I'd be back to my original status, Fawl or no Fawl to mess with me.

Freedom on the cuff—that's where I stood right now. But after a week had gone by, I heard that Fawl had been monographed to the sheriff's property room. Separate building, demotion, blow to his ego and—like so many ravenous politicians—blackberried from everything that he felt righteous in conduct about. I never knocked the vine in jails or prisons, so it was probably a blood-tight, to the point, word of truth. I felt neither good or bad about his deferment . . . just glad he wasn't around, snorting his bad breath on me or anyone else. I only wondered if he'd turn into a thief, like so many who've claimed they couldn't locate your items in stock. Luckily, I had nothing in storage, and I felt fine; just great. Maybe now I could try for the poem which would seclude the girl as being strictly my own—incorporated through all the various angles and pledges.

As I moved to my quiet room—dark, musty, the smell of an under-the-bridge case in full atomization—I was thinking of a person I'd met at a visitor's table back in prison: "You're all right Laura—I hope you'll be able to tolerate me so I can enjoy you." Hmm . . . just a staircase thought, or was it true excitement I'd been waiting to admit for awhile? Then I thought, shit, I just want to continue to benefit from something, something good.

Defer my ambitions to God, I thought. Let's check Him out and see if He can give me something to stand behind and ROAR about, the little slug. Let's see what His pike can hold with an attitude case, such as we all have when the winds blow horizontally.

Rock Salt & Glissandos

Leaving my door open and toweling it out a bit, I decided, alright, let's see about that tray the guard was keeping warm for me. I strolled like a robed priest down the stairs, took off the lid, and there it was: dark-brown, black and mangled meat, with a lump of under-cooked rice to the side. Another tray of roadkill. Only my victory helped to get it down without ralphing.

Five hours from lockdown, Morpheus would be on my mind. I'd be reaching for that textured quilt in the sky, the one that would bring me over the influence. Through all our stanzas, I thought, we all deserve it intermittently.

Instead I settled on a very thin sleep. But it was sleep, the closest thing to a family I had in there. I had no choice but to take it.

Steve Fisher

cooking film

The inmate
snaps a flash on the camera
for visitation Polaroids.

Negatives? I ask.

None, he says.

I pose with her . . .

  Shit:

    there's my woman—
  for *street* money—

  like she's been
    squirted
    from a tube
    onto
    a fun house mirror,

  lordy,

in
the mid-afternoon
desert hearth—

and me,
groin-mad
and wanting her
regardless.

Rock Salt & Glissandos

responding to prison guards

God damn
it's not anger.
It's malice,
come on motherfucker
it's rage,
it's cold

your
balls on the
walkway
your intestines
draped
around your wife
like a stole —
    hot whiskey
    the charges
    dropped
    a slow death
    enthusiastic
    witness.

Steve Fisher

methods of exile

It was a little after nine and I was the second customer in the bank, but the first to exit. I had made a deposit for my girlfriend, and with a clasp of her I.D. and a note to the teller, was able to cash a check for myself, a hundred and forty dollars worth. Since I was unable to keep up an account of my own, and since the check was from out of state, and since I lagged in so many areas of common life, it was almost a necessity to have a responsible girlfriend in a case like this, where even the managers at the all-night supermarkets wouldn't touch a check of this sort, especially having only a social form of I.D. to present. The state had my driver's license for another eight months or so, after revoking it for three years. But I've drunk so much alcohol that I don't quite remember why they took it. So now I either bussed it, or was a foot. Today, I was a foot.

   It was already over 90 degrees, a sure sign of pores opening into fever-like liquids as you moved along, along like a walking pole of short sticks, making each foot dense-up as if you apparently had a joint of toothpicks extending from your perspiring crotch, serving as transport. The city was a flat 2400', the air thin and pinching, scaled down to a gasp, but in a car you at least felt as if you were traveling. I simply moved with the sense that I had patio bricks affixed to both feet, but at least my wallet was full, finally on the side of commercial validity. Good feelings formed and extended to Sharon, my woman of nine years; good feelings were induced by the money, induced to people and circumstances that I would normally scowl at. It was a type of spiritual trickery, and being completely aware of it, let it settle on me for a brief stand of regulated self-statement.

   I headed west down Ft. Lowell, a seven-lane commuter strip choked with fungus and fumes—all quite tropical if you bothered to look upward at the palms, or sight-saw the yucca and ocotillo as they cut your skin while trudging through the make-shift dirt walk the poor provided themselves with — an unending thruway of bumpers and grills and gypsy heat, distorting the automobiles into a screen of winding waves and rising crust. The road itself went on and on, finally ending in a mirage gully. It was another lost path that Kerouac once traveled by starlight, just a dusty old farm road with a few scattered adobes back then, now hustled with every sort of drive-through and Minute-Mart and franchise the girded shoulders could support. A heavy implant, to say the least; an ego-thorned malice-mat, cold and intrusive to the passer-by.

I walked with my back to the flow of traffic. Had this thing against being seen or pointed at by oncoming cars, trucks, gasoline freights, bikes — all that *rush*, and able to be detected by anyone. A nance pointing as he went by, casing you up as some sort of scrag because you didn't have wheels. All manner of resentful thoughts, from drivers on their way to jobs they usually felt superior to . . . and well may be. But why tolerate it, especially if you felt superior to *that* attitude? I plodded through the scrub, another way of avoiding all things retardantly humanified.

About a quarter way into my three mile walk I caught the toe of my shoe on a rock the size of a tea kettle, jigged on the stones which followed — a little curbside shuffle — as my belt snarled with moisture around my waist. Instead of falling you learn how to hop, turning the ridiculous into a wheezing, barn-stomp eloquence. I cursed as an interstate Igloo truck roared by; I cursed my ineptness, my dependence, the sweat on my chin, the hole I was standing in while on top of the earth . . . all the levers and buttons I'd pushed and pulled before happening to notice they all were labeled sorrow. Almost all, that is, because there existed a high current somewhere within; the thing I would never let go of. It's almost pointless to describe, this thing which means so much — this flood of *all* — but it mostly shows up in the faces of other people when you have it joyously, and the police will never be able to make an identification, or lab you down with it. Lovely and legal. I cursed every gimmick in sight, then myself once more, to see if I could feel it. Everything but my paranoia, that is, which I felt was legit. Finally I crossed at a red light and bought a pack of smokes from a corner Mart, a place that smelled of bubble-gum and gasoline . . . and an effortless midnight welling of beer-runs and holdup attempts.

Now, of course, as I left the place, I was facing traffic as I walked. But instead of raging at the mockers, I flew inward to Gina. Gina, my faithful correspondent for over a year, with only one bad exchange to show for all the goodness and hope we rightfully knew as ours. We listened, laughed, coiled tenderly in each other's laps when the future said no and was motionless. We razzed the deformity of nearly all conduct, including ours when we deserved it. Explored homespun concepts — "Bitch Feed," "Enamel Concentration," the "Tortuous Fly" and whatever else we could bolt down to reason, our reason. "Bless the cradle and coffin," I once wrote her. "Content precedes condition."

Steve Fisher

"My office is in the cellar now," she wrote back. "The sewer line exploded and the contents are surely on their way to the coffins right now. Seems we can never get away from the shit and steam of open cracks . . . tho I see a lot of women trying to do just that by crossing their legs. But the pipeline never surrenders, right? And listening is fifty percent of plumbing. You'd belch laughter at the sounds I sure as hell do." And she would go on, as I had gone on each letter, a work of specialty molding, straight from the ends of our blood-branches. Seeing as I felt like I was dying all the time, or otherwise up for an odious, but trivial review, her pages made the gurney ride seem less like officiated trap holes and more like the colors of pure blood explanation. I adored her at times: "The therapy between your legs must be a roof-blasting experience for a dunce like me," I wrote her during one long stretch of confusion to light. "Don't think much about it," she replied, "because I've got at least ten years on you, depending on my mood." There. It wasn't even a matter of her telling me to stick with my girlfriend, since that bond was a cast form already made clear. She'd try and humor me as the blood pushed through my head until the room darkened with high frequencies and a treble grip. It almost always worked; my gut filling with roots and soil—good batter—as my geometry broke into light. She knew that not everything could be provided for at home, and the mailbox could be used to both of our advantages.

I had my shades on, picked up the pace a little as I thought about her, walking tight against a block-long apartment dwelling which actually had grass, not dirt, as some homey sort of feature out front. I clipped along, thinking: should I write her about last night? Also: there's not a whiff of green coming outa this grass. Perhaps a complex synthetic manufactured solely for Tucson by some sprinkler head? Or the army? Then I realized it was so devoid of ecological contact, here in the desert, it wasn't surprising at all there was no morning odor. Even the dogs, I figured, found it shocking enough to leave alone. Like all cities, there were deliberate modes of exile to the higher spirit, as well as to the common eye.

The cars thundered in a whirlpool of exhaust at another intersection, my eyes moistening with sweat, glare, chrome, emission clouds and cadence, until the light changed and I scurried across like a rodent. As I hit the continuous bleach of roadway on the other step of curbing, I thought time might be a matter of what physiology you happen into, regardless of how it happened. I was feeling filterlessly slow, wanting an oxygen vitamin and more lung hair. A spot out of the diesel impaction. The previous night ripped from my head. I walked on, unavoidable as the world.

Suddenly, I felt like I was making it closer to the street I wanted, like I was actually getting somewhere. And it seemed to help when I noticed a shortcut of sorts; a land port, really; just a large barren opening unfit for the wildest of natural life. I saw an alley behind it and cut on through. Wondered what they had buried underneath.

Rock Salt & Glissandos

The sound of the street faded. The chops of my feet were almost silent. I came partly out of my detention with a laugh, still glazed over like a melting donut from the sun. I dabbed at my face with the tuck-in of my shirt. Almost lit a cigarette, it being so calm but decided against it, a practice I tried to maintain while walking. Noticed the brownness all around me, except for one healthy looking green Palo Verde. It lessened the tension from my eyes on down, as if I had come into a sanctuary of sorts. I strode into the alley.

It was dirt, too. So dirt-hard, in fact, that recent tire tracks just stood out like fork pressings in a cafe pie crust. A few yellowing shrubs bent next to the brown walls that separated the alley from the property on the other side. Most of these backyards showed nothing but clotheslines and dilapidated tin sheds, but it was possible that someone had something going. Even if they didn't, why not grant them the capability?

Not far downway from me came two Mexican kids, young alley pulp, with a tight gaze as they approached. It was supposed to be bad-assed, and I recognized myself as their target right off . . . but I also saw a legitimate expression as our faces moved forward, an expression that seemed mixed with passion, triggers, and long moaning wails to walls of skin and moonlight—just an apron against the darkness—as another day of rejection dissolved on them, hard.

It fell just as hard on me, though in different methods, but there's no explaining that in the solitude extending between us. And seeing as though I was built more like a Chinese Ping-Pong player than a Safeway dumpster, I could go onward, waiting to see if they would make a move. The calm felt in the land port, almost needless to say, now tried to inflate my brain into my skull like a tire low on air, but for some reason didn't quite manage . . . and the reason was that fear was something I was used to—corning from in or from out—and I rather pushed it along in a shopping cart, just like the old women in the market who knew exactly which aisle to pass because it would cripple them. They were assured, knowing where and how to roll it along.

The kids, if you call a twenty year old a kid, had been talking quietly to themselves until we were about fifteen feet apart. Then they broke into a spat of laughter and needle-nose conversation—none of which I could understand; none of which the Department of Parks and Recreational Spanish, either, would have taught, those pavilion craft-monkeys—until one of them lifted a coke bottle over the wall with the point of his right shoe, and from there on in we were retina-to-reaction, momentarily still, waiting to play it out. It was still their move, and they didn't windbag around it.

"Give us your money, not your foodstamps!" the taller of the two said. "Now!"

I stood my ground, thinking of the harm they could do, and said nothing.

"Or do we have to pry it loose with these?"

A couple of short, wide blades appeared, business-like, almost as if I were in a bait-and-tackle shop being asked *Sir, how will these do? Fine, just fine. And*

125

Steve Fisher

could you wrap them separately?

I thought, how stupid to carry this money in my wallet, the first money I'd seen in along time. I wasn't about to go down for it, put my hands a little below my hips, an indication I was making incision of my own in them, that something would give.

"Look," I said in a voice coated with mucous, which I spit out quickly with a curled tongue, "it's too early in the morning for the type of cash you're after. On top of that, you can't beat the streets very long like this, simply because there's too many cops around. Hell, we're so close to the street you could pick up a patrol tail at any moment." They listened, just a bit mystified by my bullshit. "Also, *esé*, I'm sober as an early morning fry cook."

They faced each other with quick tongues, then back up to me.

"You say *esé*?"

"Yeh."

"Where you *been*, anyhows?" they said relaxing, fumbling with their blades like they were old-time whittlers.

"Rolled up in a sewerline, more than once."

"You mean the joint?"

"Stinks, yeah. Try 'n avoid it. Nice talkin to ya's."

"Oh yeah," they were saying as I hurried off, thinking: I do have some social instincts after all. Might have been able to tell them that the sun was an overcoat and the rain a free shower . . . but why mess up *their* free enterprise with a pointless half-bark?' I hit the street corner, noticing how the sun made rasin-wood out of the houses constructed of lumber.

I was too far in the shallows to realize how badly cut I could have been in the alley. Or injured, one way or another. I wasn't quite an idiot, though I may have been heading in that direction, but I did have a rind on me that wasn't ready to come off—just then, that is. As the world rocked violently and moments fell from the sky like spears, I bent against the exchange back there, finally approving of my wick, of the courage it took with my bones (and money) at stake, of how the odds were brutally against me *with one gangrel slip* . . . and the odd thought which could have made the bloodless difference throughout it all: that acceptance is virtually the non-questioning of what is being advanced, which in our case equaled—not canceled—the motivations we stood, and ultimately, parted with. What could have been a scarlet etching became nothing more than brief dandelion terror for me; a soft circumstance that may have backboned me into rage had I not had other igniting sighs and crippling meters, like nightmares of snakes, coming from all public, but mainly private, entrances. But I also had turf to cover with Gina; a text, nearly foregathered in the musk of daybreak from the charcoal pavings that pickled last night; a fructose Hymn with the euphoria of an all-night drink-down, along with the sorrowful truth of last-end bites. It was a muddled feeling of depraved affluence, but in the alley it was a clear advantage, soaring and sparkling down against the dusty threshold. Now it was time to tender-edge this sort of demon rash I'd developed between nightfall and daylight, integrating once more my life with hers.

    I made it back to the small apartment by 9:45, heavy, hazy, my mind full of buckshot and kelp. Just lingering there. I snapped the cooler switch on, drank some RC cola, checked my gonads for cancer lumps and tried to relax for a minute; to figure how best to lay this despondent carnival out to her. But since there seemed no top or bottom to this flare going through me, I whipped out the typer, let it sit there at finger level before me, then began laughing at the history of my ignorance. I was about to add to it, and it didn't bother me a bit. Besides, if I sent the thing off to Gina, she might just read it as a vague afterimage; a butter-vision postmarked from a field of mutton while staring into the colors of an old plane's propeller while it got ready for a low-elevation run across the border. And since I didn't have to send it to her, it made no difference in allocution or forms of adagio carols. Starway or windpipe hangover I rolled a sheet of paper in, and began punching the keys in even, metric torture. Whatever came out, as a result of last night's wild floppings, was sure to be a rough fare . . . but what of it? It's been long known that desperation supersedes rationality. I didn't bother to headline the thing. I just dove in:

    Been preoccupied with manic emotions and hell . . . nothing unusual with that, but wondering about it is: why does this hang me; why the continuous smudging and glare, the bile dripping into heavy disfigurement so often, cinereous, centerless in my blood my cranium the works? Then a few peaceful moments, at times under the heaviest of influences: calm reasoning, knowing that things such as palm trees aren't really going to fly away, that they're real. Sure, the pressure's more intense than the heat these days, or so it seems: it's been a hell of an internship, mildly speaking . . . but this goes back through the years, long before my hard-ons became spiteful at times, or even tender gestures which resulted in betrayal from snapping hens . . . in a way, it's been like living in a dozen universes in a body so inefficient, so intolerant that arms and limbs are absurd mockings – natural gimcracks – so incomplete they ridicule the jack-like ends of these multiple worlds, these barbells attached to crossing toothpicks, straining to stiff each other and separate me from a singular fate.

    But whatever it is I'm talking about, these are some of the reasons I turned to books and writing in the first place. And now, at four a.m. darkness, the sun dangling beneath our head of the earth like a neck-shearing medallion, coming off weeks of inspirational slam, it seems like the time to question this madness; this pool of sweat when my palms are turned upward, as it were, is at hand. Maybe discover a solution, a thing that all of now will be satisfied with: like that first solitary smoke and shower, six days after a petty arrest . . . plus a change of sheets and blues as well (and you don't ever have to be in lock-up to feel the now of that). But I really despise opening my rib cage and letting the sour mash pump out in scurvied huddles, as indecipherable as a coded schoolboy ledger. The older G. knows something of what I'm saying, regardless of the fact that my clarity, if any, isn't coming from the crisper. And from the musical and lit bios I've read, these people tossed and turned with

Steve Fisher

inward prowl, heaving with the mulch I'm foolishly trying to explain . . . not only to you, but to the darkness: the darkness was once on my side, sensuous against my skin, but it too has become gel and swelter, swollen with Hamtramck bristles and razor outlines of sycophants, harnessed in flame. But you know I find myself among a majority on almost any page of bio, and find explanation a rotten form of breaking into light . . . but a fine way of lousing things up, like mixing brain cells with smegma and forming another concrete lobe.

But at this point, this open-net now, I'm gambling with both. Also myself. And I'm thinking that maybe you, Gina, have been through some of the same gates; can commune with my holdbacks, whatever they are. Understand in fashion what a few of your sentences could cover: roll it off and have me laughing at my fears, even on an airless night like this. And since my fears are like a pyramid of cabinet roaches, plentiful and scattering, I don't bother anyone with them. Just you, tonight in gentle tones. In fact, I can't bother anyone with them: the do-the-job, what's-for-supper, problemless sleepers HAVE no real metaphysical/spiritual, even pondering questions about the lug-nuts I'm on fire with, so it can be difficult, awkward, etc., just sitting down with them, trying to act normal. (And with the exception of baseball, most people think of my remarks, or questions, as totally off-color. Course, it's true to an extent — I don't sit well at Formica counters under fake leather stools for very long, even if it is the girlfriend's kickbacks I'm attending. And once in awhile I give in, thinking of myself as a misdeal of sorts — tho I wouldn't swap this hand for another — until a gnarl shuts the gathering phaseless, and I chuck the idea of a misdeal, but I wonder where the true flesh is with her. Or maybe I know, since there's not much complexity or intrinsic wailing going on. You know, it's like trying to party with a roomful of tombheads. The sedate like a voice, that — in analogy — comes from a speaker with a loose magnet. I like a voice of ember and boulevards and frost on the wings of sandpipers; a voice across the junk on a table, lapsing into eternity, with a hard and colorful hue. That's something I understand, because I learn from energy. That's why your letters count, as if snagged from a flying oasis. And I'll be the first to admit my dense gargle, but maybe I've found an answer to my brooding: seclusion without * * * * *; the percentage of hand-stitched light I can only get from a few people, and only one here in town. Should give him a call, get together if he isn't pressed or henched-in. His head tingles like the snow up top a sunlit mountain; he's full of weather, like me. But stable, somehow, guided by the rote of independence . . . and never outraged by my conduct, humor, visions . . . butt-buddies, you know? fifteen years, meeting in a roominghouse where I was the janitor, sweeping outside his door one afternoon. By seven p.m. we were drunk on wine, in a non-stop butterbreath that hasn't stopped yet for anything. Integrated waves. Imagine you have a friend or two like this, a solar chime . . . so I'll quiet down now, but feel free to comment if you noticed anything, if you're up to it, and your thoughts haven't deepened to a tapestry of heaven and sludge. That would be explanation, not definition. Just bare in mind I thought these emotions belonged here with you tonight, so regard this as confidential and privileged, hahaha-ha, ok? — And shouldn't I have stuck a ")" in there somewhere? Ah well, some cities don't even have sewers, and many landlords are more *efficient vandals than schoolboys with rocks. Be well, fresh fruit and all,* and I signed my name very articulately, looking something like what moose prongs would scrawl into a drying mud bank.

I lowered my eyelids on the pages for a moment, wondering what I had just done, then came to life and wrote "Gina" across the first page, guessed at the date, then addressed the thing off to her, using my next-to-last stamp.

My tongue bled all over the stamp, and it smeared the envelope in a whisk. I thought perfect, a trailblazer in red, then headed out to find a mailbox.

Steve Fisher

somewhere there's a coffin with a soft blue lining

80% of the world is starving and
America's on a diet.

Where can we go?
What's left
to sell to the bushwhackers?
Why is the price
so low and
the world flat now, unsignificant?

I count, but there's difficulties
including you —

   the years, O fuckers, the years . . .

Curled in a ball of terror,
a form begins that
one day will

auger through you.

Rock Salt & Glissandos

thermal hibernation

Mercy had fled like a round of buckshot.
Like the last folk you'd
 finally repulsed.

Mercy had been tattooed on me for a week though
 like heavy steel mesh, blessed
  before battered
and affixed.

Kissing the woman always of jasmine
 well—
 she tasted of fuel line
and cut-rate glup;
 roach water.
I simply didn't miss this forthcoming smear—
ensnared in classical barbell trinity
 and playlist,
the stonebar fleshed me out; cool, easy
 game; dropping
  coals in my focal pods
until I pressed against old habits
 beloved and illegal;
the soft quill of Junior Modern.
 I had been reformed
and now saw what a slob job is done—
off by a second, like an idiot's trumpet.

 Going back, back
before my head became loud—LOUD like being trapped
 in a dishwashing HOBART, all was sonorous.
My body—before JUMPING like a wino
 forced at gunpoint not to piss—was jacked-up in beauty hooks,
old trellis displays and lilac railing.
Thoughts appeared intoned like islands; like
 peddle harpsichord snake plugs,

Steve Fisher

    basted walking ribs all
colored like the off-duty flagman who controlled
   the switches
until a blowgland carried them off like rose wings
   to vaults sealed in padlock.
     The arfy-darfy. Something
like over-salted wisdom, burning itself
   to death
the more I tried reviewing what I wanted to retain.

After's I shook — my concentration, silk sweet veins . . .
   vertebra and all my stems. *Burning tongue*. Lungs
swinging, hacking brownness up like ice cubes.
   Trounced. Ranting triggers.

Needed was the saddling only a good opiate mount would enunciate.

Candleshrine.

Nodding inscriptions.

House plants phased with stage lights. That
   sort of thing. Bulgarian
     folk music.

Special services unavailable.

Mercy fled from the face of the earth.
   I felt a receding &
God was probably a hell of a skip tracer.

Rock Salt & Glissandos

windy gray

I waited on the bus at classification this time, knowing enough about Arizona prison yards to realize I'd soon be wading through a lot of bleak shit. I'd been fingerprinted, photographed and old-techniqued, then filed into a passage-tank where I stood under a half light. They had about thirty of us, chained by footlink in twos, our wrists cuffed to leather hip belts. Another twelve were being processed in the movement room, which we could see through the small, thick observation window in our area. I looked away. I clasped my hands. I stared at the painted concrete, which had been chipped and cut with steel bracelets. I felt the aloof tension trapped in the room and thought of huge, powerful, ugly machines at construction sites: scraper plows, bulldozers, cranes. I felt little of the earth or the world.

From a lesser eye, in fact, had come a statement that I do time for apparently feeling so little of society. For participating in a manner that was outside of the structure. Yet the fantastic truth, as if blown from a Coltrane tenor, was far above our daily courtroom breach: I'd felt so much of the common clause, feathering around me, that the response was to evade the balm of street custody and go with the grip of my own head . . . which, of course, is downplayed as a secondary function of life in some circles. I did it with drugs that were regulated into strict medical, along with a total mixture of booze and emotion. Damn right it made a difference. Though when Coltrane cleaned the junk from his system, locked in the bedroom at his request, he was fortunate enough to have his mother bring water. I'd jones in the jail, throwing wet toilet paper at the cold and ferocious air vent, nightmares pumping out of me like poison darts from a blowgun. No doubt we both held something, in us and astral, linked to a deep and warmer humanity. Everything else was a mechanism of custom.

I was, at any rate, alive in a slug's September. But I might as well have been

Steve Fisher

in an unknown month on an uncharted planet, for that was the flat alien rush of my brotherhood: obscure, like industrialized human deadware. Even the blacks—who, as a group, are constantly loud and lunging—caught the thrust of blood in their throats at this point. I could appreciate the ride for that, yet here I was—a flash fire in the music—tied to an old and liver-fat granny rapist with slimy, pointy hair. And, like an old fart, he geezed: layers of fat on his soft wrinkled hands, and a stump neck, squat, under rows of chin hang. A froth had settled in one corner of his mouth, then these thick, binocular glasses that shot his pupils out like boot eyes. He was revolting. And everyone milled away from us, certainly with good reason: he wheezed a nasty, repugnant salisbury breath, a hot reeking craw in a fixless room.

I wasn't the only mismatched con in that cell. Yet no one else was footlinked to a geezer who raped the old women who were confined in nursing homes. I was stuck, and accepted it as some bizarre form of logic: apparently, it had to do with justice. But we all had to do with justice, *mandatory* justice for the most part, which by now was nothing new. What was new, at least to me, was the fact I'd be going to the same joint as this freak. Otherwise, we'd have been issued separate seats on the bus. Yet what kind of mind would consider us as being of the same ilk?—that was another question lost in the Box of Black.

For once, however, the wait was short. They shot some electricity through a rear wall of the cell and we walked out—we *hobbled* out, tearing up our shins and ankles—a back door of the holding block that had a step over that a few people tripped on. But the whole system was rigged with blocks and we either knew it, or anticipated as much, and plotted other ways to get around. There was, really, no other choice. So when the aging D.O.C. coach showed up there was no point in expecting much. Again, a short wait in the Phoenix dawn, as cardboard boxes of our stuff were loaded on. We had a toothbrush, a comb, a couple of dirty T-shirts. The envelopes and stamps I once had had been stolen from the property room back in the Tucson jail. There were no inmate employees in that corridor of the building. We boarded the coach, still wearing our state-issued shower shoes.

But the bus had been modified into a 42nd Street grotto. They had a separation cage designed up front, housing tear gas, and shotgun seats, for the guards to sit on. The cage was made with regular police wire, but the weave was a bit looser than the mesh covering our windows. We could see out of them, to an extant, but the light that came through was the type that almost, but not quite, illuminated color. Then they had ripped out the standard seating and replaced it with these little, molded schoolboy seats, like the kind that at one point had an arm flap. Since I led the way in my party, I moved toward a window seat like it was the only option we had. The decrepit old fuck just sloshed his fat in the aisle and stood dumb for a moment—which was too long, in our situation—so I turned into the seat, clenched my tendon, and snapped our footline with a volt. As his eyes popped, I said, "Sit down." He sat down softly, rather like a hippo submerging its ass in shallow water, and I pictured him sliding into bed with granny saying dirty childish things.

We were in a touring jail now, idling while the guards got their coffee, their weapons in order:

"Then that's your coffee?"

"That's my coffee with the sugar, and this is my gun."

"Well, I know that's your gun, but I thought we had our coffees secured."

"My cup is the cup indicated by the square handle."

"Okay, then this is my cup, with the black coffee. Is it still hot?"

"It's still hot. Did DeForest top off the gas tank?"

"I don't know. I thought Officer Lid was in charge of vehicle operations."

"Well, he's having a coffee with Sergeant Crow at the moment."

I leaned against the window grill, thinking what a fiasco my jacket must be. My file. Then the whole bus rocked as the driver stepped on. Never had I seen a cop this big. He could have worn a manhole cover as a belt buckle. The other two guards moved from his way, just smiling, with loping, red ears. The driver looked back at us, poised and rough. Then somebody in front of me spoke on an idea.

"Hey, *fuck* you, punk!"

The two guards looked up, thinking that they heard another voice.

"Motherfuckin' *punk* thinks he's *tough*."

"Take but five of us to hold him, while the rest of you go up in him."

The cage door opened with a crash, the driver kicking his footsteps down the run.

"All RIGHT," he said, "just who wants to tell me that to my face? HUH? Who's MAN enough to ADMIT what he just said?"

Nobody moved. Stupidity vs. silence. But he was right in front of *me*, for some reason, staring down like I had it coming. Maybe he didn't like the company I kept.

"I'll take off my badge, and fight man-to-man."

More of the same.

"Motherfuckers," he said. "You let me know when you're ready. I'll pull the goddamn bus off to the side of the road."

He walked back and slammed the cage door, probably thinking he'd won the battle. Of course the only thing he'd won, if you'd take *that* kind of a victory, was the simpering respect of his fellow officers.

But the mood on the bus relaxed. Not much, though enough to make room for little exits in the hold. It meant a certain flexibility within the immediate, instead of frozen responses to authoritative commands. It meant that the edge can go both ways. It meant that it does. It meant FUCK YOU, and get this train a-rolling. About five minutes later the gates swung open and we pulled out: Phoenix was a mad glare of suntanned hang overs, puking and squealing and grinding the roads. It made the street cops mad, because there weren't enough laws on the books to effectively put the entire city behind bars.

Yet.

"Are we going?" the geezer asked me. He was impatient, oily. I turned away.

I looked out the window, glad to be leaving the maximum security of Alhambra. Alhambra was, roughly, the custody level used for apes. They had told me I'd be going to a medium joint in the area, but they lie: we were on our way to the southeast corner of the Great State of Arizona, stopping first at the walls, Florence, followed by a smaller camp outside of Tucson. They'd drop some off, and pick others up along the way. But this routine shuttle was a totally hell-bent journey for some of the people sitting around me, though for others, including myself, it was simply part of the procedure.

We rolled on. We dropped off twenty, picked another ten up at Florence. I watched one guy get off and piss the bus into laughter. I mean, it ran down the front of his jump suit, marking him as easy prey at the Florence reception center. But the guy looked to be close to twenty-five years old: hadn't he been anywhere in his life? Probably not, like the geezer beside me, except down to the grade school between paper plates of soft food. I cracked my neck and sunk into my shoulder blades as if they were pillows, noting the small, prefab courthouse that had been connected by tunnel to the prison. It was a bright, fruity red, all trimmed in white, and contrasted with a marker flag run up a short pole. Inside it was rigged with a pro tem judge and a Bible.

The bus crackled along. But the huge cop drove at about 30 mph, making the trip feel endless as we passed the Florence graveyard. It was filled with small, wooden sticks, that crossed around knee level, finally tooled in black with your state number: if you died in prison before your sentence expired, you were buried out there while the state collected money on your corpus. The law said it wasn't a scam. But all those sticks made me really think of groups, of people collected around one central notion then pawned off as an assembled whole. It was wrong, it didn't work, yet it explained why the days were regulated into monocore: individualism was simply too far above the plan. But the graveyard soon faded, and again we were on the slow, rolling route through the desert.

I managed to sleep for awhile, waking on the interstate not far from Tucson. We stopped at the prison, barely lucky enough to get water and a sack lunch: a sort of latex cheese on white bread, which we bent to our hands in order to eat. More were dropped off, more stepped on, including one of my pardners from previous times. He took a seat across the aisle from me, his muscles cut and angled from working out on the weight pile. He was doing a natural for first degree murder.

"Killer," I said.

Killer circled his eyes around the bus, making a tight face.

"*Stinks* on this bus, don't it," he said. "What is that smell, anyway?"

I wasn't sure either, but it was sickly sweet and fingered with flesh. It

Rock Salt & Glissandos

forced you to choke. It forced you to gag.

"Seems to be commin' from up front, from those Dunkin' Donuts an' shit those cops be swillin'," said the guy in front of us, musing at the way the cops worked both the donuts *and* coffee with their tan caps laid off on the ammo compartment. "OUGHTA GET A PORTER ON HERE TO MOP UP THIS STINKING SHIT!" he yelled.

The guards simply looked and grinned aimlessly, light from the windshield reflecting in their tall, steel foreheads.

"Where you headed?" I asked Killer.

"They told me Douglas. But then, they've told me a lot of things," he said.

"Only shit I've heard about Douglas is bad," I said.

"Heard right. No recreation, no books in the library . . . hope I can find a job, doing something besides raking rocks."

"Is that the issue?"

"Unless you have a trade," he said.

"Douglas," I said.

"Shit."

"If these ruddy ducks ever stop chewing, that is, and move the bus along."

"FIRE THIS MOTHERFUCKER ONTO THE ROAD," said the guy up front. "YOU'RE KEEPING MY FRIENDS WAITING you stupid water-runs-off-the-neck like rubber-necked motherfuckers."

The guards just ignored it. But Killer glanced at my seatmate, whose eyes pointed downward.

"Stand up and get in my collar once," Killer told me.

I stood up, shifted, as Killer leaned across the aisle. I got a cigarette from his collar. I dropped it in his lap, as he pulled a striker and matches from the fluff in his shirt.

"I heard they were taking all matches, on account of somebody making a bomb," the geezer said nervously.

"More than one way to make a bomb," said Killer, blowing smoke under the seat. "More than one way to light a smoke, too."

He coughed, then passed the cigarette across the aisle. I dragged heavily, said, "Killer."

"Finish it," he said. "I had one before I got on."

I rolled it in my fingers, lazily, as the bus circled the camp and pulled out. There went the fence, the razor ribbon, the yards, towers and cameras. The guards in the shack on the lip of the road. In a few minutes we were back on the interstate, contemplating our futures, that one small mistake that brought us here far behind the highway and logo we traveled on now. The cigarette burned. And I noticed the dust settling upon the jump suit of the geezer, watched as it deflected off the grease on his head.

"Let me hit some of that before you put it out," he said.

His lips worked the air like a scum-sucking fish, and he looked wretched. But he was cuffed to my right ankle like we were enjoined Siamese convicts.

I guessed his music was on the order of rubber-sheeted cradle-tones.

"I'll give you shorts," I told him, quiet-like. I took a few more pulls, very leisurely, then passed him the filter load. He sucked it down like a slobbering hog. I curled back into my space, but Killer sat open eyed, straight up, awaiting it all. He hadn't yet considered who my seatmate was.

"First vacation I've had in years," Killer said, calm and relaxed.

"Then there's Douglas, around the corner."

"Yeah, there's that."

We rode on, passing the landmarks along the highway. Red Rock, the Cochise Stronghold. Traffic thinned the farther south we got, and a billboard for THE THING? began appearing. Killer, now a stone-cold correctional tourist, looked through the grating and remarked to me, in profile:

"Arizona. They say you come as a tourist, and leave on parole."

I laughed. It was the first thing that had made sense to me all day.

"They come looking for work, too," I said, "but the employers have already bailed out."

"This state just be runnin' scam after scam," said the guy up front, and somebody across from him said, "*Yeah* they are."

We got off the main road sometime early in the afternoon, and onto a minor highway which hosted a number of phony retirement villages. I saw a bank, an office, a few other things, more pre-fab shit that went up in a day. Not far from this was our turn off: another dirt road, maybe five-thousand feet above sea level. The bus drove in for about three-and-a-half miles, a caddie at the gate finally stopping us for paperwork. We sat, we lingered. Then we pulled away from him, twisting in our seats, some of the youngsters flashing the bird. We entered the special hanger for arrivals and stopped, looking out through our windows, at the concrete the girders the pressed steel. We paid attention to the few inmates walking around in there, to see if they smiled or not. Some of them did, so we looked beyond the faces, wondering why.

But the bus had been parked on a deliberate embankment, so there was a curbing to hop that went deeper than our foot-links. The driver just stood there, facing us, hands on his hips; hat tipped, extremely pleased. I told the geezer to put his foot out, to give me some chain, but the guards were yelling "MOVE IT! MOVE IT!" and he wasn't paying attention. The gross motherfucker was listening to the cops.

"Stick your foot over the edge," I told him again.

He wavered, then looked at me.

"Like this?" he asked, crouching his foot outward.

I made the leap, followed by the geezer, and the driver instructed us to form a line opposite the bus. I glanced at the spot and saw Killer. We hobbled over.

A couple of guards were taking the cuffs off, but in front of us sat a whole table of the brownsuits. Others rolled dollies of our stuff up, to the table, where it was then processed and marked on a sheet of our possessions. I was

Rock Salt & Glissandos

thankful to be moving. To work my legs, my bones, to inhale the huge place and to rub at the small of my back. And to get away, finally, from chaplick. He stood by one of the rear tires on the bus, silent, fearful. Alone. Cunted. I waited, with Killer, on the next move.

"I gotta take a piss," he said, looking around.

"Likewise," I told him.

Folks were getting off the bus, crowding the area we stood in. Carbon monoxide choked the space. Killer leaned over, confidentially.

"This way," he said, walking across the room.

He had checked out a wall, a few doors, to make sure of the one we'd be entering. To make sure of the exact door. In this case, the head. It was a matter of protocol: a mistake in the trivial webbing of the joint was the thing that would cost you, the thing you constantly had to be looking out for. So as Killer led, I followed. We both knew the footing. The guards were watching, though they otherwise ignored us.

But everyone awoke to the flushing. They came, circulating, many looking at each other for the first time. I was called to the property table and issued state clothing: jeans, T-shirts, socks, brogans, a few disposable razors. I was told to stand behind a curtain and try the pants on, just this little hang of sheets in the center of the room. I got a feel of how large the contrivance was: like putting a tarp over the city of Akron, or something like that. And here we had this stall, this little sheet that fluffed as your elbows caught it in movement. I walked out, over to the property counter. An old convict was dispensing our state shit.

"These jeans must be about ten sizes too long," I told him, and they were. Probably too long for a stilts-walker as well.

"That's all we got right now," he told me, resting a hand on the counter. "We're out of things."

His old hair glowed like foil sprinkled in orange sauce. A brown tooth slanted across his mouth, chipped and cut long ago. I looked at him, but as easily natured as possible. I had an idea.

"I'll kick down some tobacco, come state pay," I told him.

He looked me over. His hand still rested on the counter.

"Let me see if they brought the new issue," he said. "Some was dued in."

He walked into the long rows of shelving and I waited. I noticed these short, stocky girls, seated at another table, both of them darkened with facial deformities: they were only institutional nurses, not actually certified to care for people. I was called over and told to sit down.

"Who do we have here?" one of the nurses asked the other.

"Five eight two zero two," said the one with my jacket. "Ask him to roll up his sleeve."

"Now, roll up your sleeve for me," the first one said. "That's it."

She took my blood pressure and asked if I had ever used drugs intravenously. In fact, they had a prepared sheet of roughly twenty questions, a

Steve Fisher

cat-and-mouse list I was required to respond to. To respond to correctly. I could be dying of cancer, but that would only burden the department—the state—so I watched their tar-like facial contours replying "no" to the questions. They wrote my answers on a little card and sent me off. But I had noticed an avocado-sized growth on the ankle of the one with my file. It bobbled in her pantyhose when she shifted on the chair. I thought, this is what the geezer had been after, only worse. I walked back to the property counter. My issue was there, sitting off to the side. "State pay," I told the old convict.

"Alright," he said.

"Thanks, Holmes."

Killer walked over, a young guy whose forehead was half tan from wearing bandannas with him. "Ain't that Borden," he asked, "that dude you come down with?" A kind of assurance polished his eyes.

"Yeah," I said. I recognized one of the tattoos on his arm.

"Looks like we're all goin' to the same unit, the Mohave Unit," he said. "We'll get him later on."

He was looking over my shoulder, this head of curly, brown hair dancing around.

"I think he figures as much," I said. Killer just stood there, digging on his fingernails, nose down. It was his way of paying attention.

"Don't matter," said the other guy. "He'll be off this yard by tonight."

The guy walked off. But slowly, steadily, like he was pulling a loaded barge behind him.

"I knew that dude from South Unit," said Killer. "He's all right."

"Rip Borden a new asshole, I don't doubt that," I said.

"ALL RIGHT, LISTEN UP!" yelled one of the guards. "THESE INMATES ARE TO ASSEMBLE AGAINST THE REAR WALL. WHEN YOU HEAR YOUR NAME, LINE UP IN THE BACK!"

About fifteen names were called, including mine and Killer's. South Unit and the geezer also lined up.

A long white van splattered with mud soon arrived, and all of us boarded with our grip of state-issue. Only now, at *this* point, we were instructed to remove our shower clogs and put on our state boots. Our brogans. Everyone dove in like a bag of mad snakes, the van rocking, shaking, bouncing up and down. Who thinks up this ridiculous shit? Where do they school these bastards, anyway? Killer and I sat in a rear molding of the van, observing the mundane sideshow of it all. But there was also a small, darkened window back there: I tried looking at the camp as the van rolled along, at the maze, the pit of my new home.

But there was little to see except land. Just flat, yellowing miles of sun-stroked desert, unsuited to human sustenance. A water tower with fading red checks loomed up, followed by perimeter fencing and numbered security cameras. Then a rifle tower and slowly, as the van crept forward, a series of gates leading to a wirework funnel. I saw a housing unit, barely, the window cutting it from all but a brown smear. We hit a checkpoint and idled, as more gates were opened: "I'd be a misdemeanor in every other state," I heard someone say. We rolled past the checkpoint and stopped. They opened our door in a hurry, as if they had suddenly been rushed, to a small patrol of guards looking seriously arrogant. They just stood before us, sipping coffee, most of them with radios squawking from their belt holders. The order was to get out.

We got out and looked around, leaving our boxes in the van. Sure enough, another wall. But the feeling was that I'd been climbing walls all my life. Numbers were read, people lined up, but when my name was called they simply handed me my box. I stood, not quite looking at their faces.

"Dorm number ten," I was told by a young cop, then let into the yard through a small, outside door.

"Catch up with you later," I heard Killer say. I looked, for some reason, into the sky, and saw the moon sailing along near the horizon.

The gate closed behind me, and I stood on a little sidewalk. I looked across the camp past the softball field, to the yard office, the pre-fabs, the chow hall. The yard, itself, was mostly dirt. And the residents were everywhere, wearing cheap denim jackets. I was out there alone. It was chilly. Cold. Windy gray. The clouds scraped along like industrial portraits. Above the guards, in towers, watched us from their glass cages. But the dorms were numbered and spread out along the perimeter, to enclose three-quarters of the yard. Through the other quarter stood the fences, the razor ribbon and motion sensors. At least the ones I could easily see. And my new house, by the opening, exactly kitty-corner from where they had let me out. I looked, and noticed the walkway went around. I started walking, slowly, toward the fence and away from the dorms, where everyone hung out. Leering. I felt those brogans laced to my feet: they were like wearing tree stumps through a slosh pond, in the rain, hungover. The box was under my arm.

I hit the dorm without looking back. The day room and guard cage were right there, but I had the feeling of being cramped. Of having no distance, no play, with my limbs. A table of inmates dealt poker on one side and others sprinted, caps on backwards, going in and out of the door. It smelled cold, like a garage loaded with wet concrete slabs. The noise circled in a whirlpool and the lights glared like silver. I acted unimpressed, knowing. The only way to handle it. Folks hit on me for cigarettes, their faces whirring like table fans. But I didn't have any smokes. I only wanted to get settled. I wanted to find one for myself, and get a mattress from the house cop. I saw him sitting there, in the cage.

"I need a mattress," I told him.

He led me to a storage closet, sucking on his cheeks, like it was the greatest task in the world. He gestured his keys over the mattresses, stiff with authority.

"You're issued the top mattress," he said, "and one of these pillows."

I lifted the top mattress, a very thin, sad-looking bedroll. It'd be like sleeping on slimy steel, I thought. I looked back at him, not quite enraged.

"This one's all flat and farted out," I said.

The next one down was about an inch thick, really plush.

"If you have a problem with your back or something, alert medical," he said. "I have you down for one mattress."

The prick.

I threw the mattress over my shoulder and stuck a pillow on my box. He led me to the cage and stopped.

"Run E, bed thirty. If you need anything or have problems, notify me."

He handed me a combination lock. I studied his nose, which was shaped, oddly, like a tiny roller skate. He was writing about me in the log book. I turned and saw Killer. The feeling was good, like that of finding money in pants you were going to throw out. But behind him stood Borden, a rotund, geezing mass.

"A loud house just ain't a home," said Killer, looking around. "Must be some funky-assed gladiator school they're running."

"Yeah, and I'm up the E run."

"Alright," he said, setting down two boxes. I noticed the guard, who seemed to be looking at Killer with disdain, like he was late for a senseless appointment. I turned.

I grabbed the door to the E run and walked in, adjusting my eyes, the mattress slipping around on my shoulder. The run was just a cold concrete rectangle, with vents and a small window over the two-man cubicles. It was stuffy. And bed thirty was really fucked-up, on the corner across from the bathroom and showers. Televisions and radios played. I was ignored as two inmates — one black, the other white — stood across from my cell, arguing.

"No room *left* for you on this run," the white guy was saying.

"No room for *you*, you mean! I gots friends in high places roun' here!"

"*You* got friends in high panties! Now roll your shit on outta this ramp."

"I'll be back," said the black guy.

"Better bring more than a popsicle."

The black guy steamed out the door (which was also next to my cube), as I threw the mattress on my bunk. I had a line on the E run: discipline, fish, guys straight from the hole . . . what a crowd! There was a small metal locker to throw your shit into, but the door on mine was all bent to hell. Shit, I decided, they can steal my T-shirt, if they want. I was tying my sheets down when Killer walked in. I hadn't noticed, but he arrived with four boxes. South Unit was carrying the other two.

"Alright," said Killer, as he passed me.

He threw his crap on a bunk a few houses down. What jolted me, however, was Borden: the motherfuckers not only were filling up our wing, but had assigned him the vacancy right there in my cube. Unbelievable, really, yet these things always happened to me. He put his box down and sat on the

Rock Salt & Glissandos

bunk's metal, his mattress flopping at the other end. He whined for a cigarette. I suddenly thought, for some reason, of a soot-winged pigeon bearing young in a cold storefront.

"Just let me get one offa ya, buddy, I'll pay you back," he said.

I dropped my lock on the bed. I didn't want to be around him.

"Maybe that guard can help you," I told him, then went down to Killer's for one of his rollies. South Unit looked past me, up the ramp. He looked anxious.

"We're gonna get your cellie tonight," he said, as I rolled up the Bugler. I licked on the paper, then made a flicking gesture to Killer with my thumb.

"Try not to dirty my sheets," I replied.

South Unit only said "Later," and took off. Killer handed me his lighter and I lit up, smoking, kicking around his place until count. There was really nothing else to do at this point: over three-hundred miles on the D.O.C. bus. Borden just sat on his bunk, scratching. The cold September night was coming on.

We were walking back after chow, me and Killer, Killer looking at the weight pile, inquisitive and silent. The wind blew upon us like the after rush of an express truck, but as I started across the sidewalk I found that the yard was a huge bowl of mud. Yet two guards were in the middle of the field, throwing rocks at one another. They seemed to ream each other with high-pitched giggling. It was sick, nauseating, at least to my ears. Killer looked at them, startled, a cup of coffee from the chow hall in his hand. Coffee was served black.

"Don't have no sugar at your house?" he asked me.

"No stash of any sort," I told him. He paused, looking at the guards.

"Wonder if we could get 'em to shoot each other," he said. "Maybe they play with silverware?"

"Maybe they'll just freeze into the yard like military statues," I said. "Seems the weather will go that far."

Killer looked at me and said, "Chilly out here, ain't it?" and took another pull on his coffee.

He was quiet as we walked, just the moonlight shining down on the guards and a lone flagpole. Coltrane might've dug this: there were riffs, modulations out here, though I started thinking there was a catch to the moon. I buttoned the collar of my jacket, and felt the first cut on my feet from the brogan leather. Incarceration, I began thinking, is largely a matter of tortures being applied to your flesh and to your sanity. The trick would be to get over.

I found my cellie just sitting there when we got back, his mattress still curled on one end of the bunk. His eyes kind of wandered, like he didn't quite know where he was. It sure wasn't the rest home. His fat head bobbled, wobbling on that stump neck, his greasy face about the color of a string mop. I passed him by, and Killer turned on the lamp at his house. His personal lamp. Otherwise, the dorm was like ash. He sat down the coffee and pulled out a book, *Small Engine Repair*, and was explaining it to me when South Unit walked in. South Unit had three others with him. They went right over to my cellie, one standing guard at the door. The house cop was nowhere in sight.

"Sure as shit, that's him," I heard one of South Unit's pardners say.

"Dude's a fuckin' *cho*-mo," said the other. "Or he's a *reverse* cho-mo, what the hell, it's almost worse than a child molester. Look at him!"

Borden cowered, feeling for a grip on the bunk.

"Starting to feel uncomfortable?" South Unit asked him. "*Huh?*"

"Listen, fellas," Borden began.

It started with fists and feet, then one of them grabbed my lock and pounded on his skull. TVs were turned down and everyone looked on, eager, completely aware of who Borden was. The bunk crashed along with his weight, Borden's screams echoing like a crow's at the mouth of a cave. This happened fast, tag team, almost as if rehearsed. Finally there was a deep, gagging inhalation, and somebody ran through the door yelling "*Cholos! Cholos!*" I watched South Unit and the others split out the back as three cops stormed in. They stood over Borden and worked their radios, calling the tower for instructions. Nobody even bothered with medical.

"This shit had it coming," I heard one of the cops say. Everything around me confirmed that.

But Borden was now bleeding all over. He was a total mess. He seemed to be breathing, yet otherwise he was out of it. And equivalent to his worth? Jesus, who knew. But it did cross my mind that the street population rather approved of this work, though it wasn't something admitted to very often. Killer turned his television on. He kept the sound off, and didn't look at the pictures.

The cops asked around before leaving. Nobody, however, had seen anything on our run. Borden was wheeled to a van they had just parked, outside, and I went to check on my bed. The bed was alright, but the cubicle wall was now flooded with blood. And so was the floor. Unfit and possibly diseased, I thought, and I went out to find a cop. The son of a bitch told me to mop it up.

I put my jacket on and went over to the yard office. A pack of guards sat around, like Great Danes but without the dignity, and I tried making a case for a new cell.

"Imagine where Borden was before he got caught," I told the Major. "Can you really expect me to stay in there?"

He nodded. He requested a housing list from a female guard, who then hopped through the office like her feet were birdsprings. She handed the Major a piece of paper. The Major gave us the orders: "Unit twelve, A-twenty." That was better than expected, since twelve was an established dorm. I walked over, looked in. I wanted to see if there was any blood on the wall. I also wanted to check out my new cellie, and make sure there weren't any mistakes this time.

There weren't.

The run was fairly quiet, and the lockers had been constructed out of unfinished wood. Bed twenty was down the ramp, away from the traffic and some of the noise. I smelled pot, hash, and heard a guitar softly playing. My new cellie was on his bed, drawing with a set of colored pencils. I saw a large picture of a naked woman: her hair was flowing, her lips were parted, the legs were out. My cellie relaxed, concentrating on his work. He told me he sold regular portraits around the yard.

"I can get a motherfucker looking just right," he said. "I can get him a penpal, when he writes to the sex ads."

"I'll have to check out the ads," I told him.

He kept drawing. I noticed a green plant in a noodle can sitting on my locker, and a mattress, thick, laid out on the bed. I was ready to move in. I headed out, on the walk, for my stuff.

But that moon.

There was something about it that made me stop and stare over the long, blowing yard. It was a different moon than the bus ride north, though I didn't know how that logically could be. But we were right on the border of Mexico, down where people and the land have changed. And that moon seemed to have changed with the latitude: it was just barren, a reminder; and spooky, because it appeared that you'd never get away from it. It hung in the sky and it hung in the sky becoming, on thought, a distance of meaningless comprehension. You could look at it and look at it and look at it. Then, you could look at it, hours apart, and still see it hanging in the same place, and most of the time nearly quartered. On that foreside, tilted, which shined like a waxed skull.

Down here, the moon always hangs in the sky.

I stood on the walk and looked out, across the compound. I now had a new house. And a strangely improvisational lifestyle, though it had always been a question of meters, of beats. It had been a long three-hundred miles: I breathed slow, breathed deeply, relaxing a bit, bodily quite shorter than that of my true extension. A lone mud-splattered guard passed me on the track, in the moonlight: I moved along to roll up.

Steve Fisher

my friends are the next generation of ants

I think of them on this weary occasion: nibbled down,
blunted, roving the dirt tract before me

   tweaked.

Touched. Entozoan. Mud life. A strangely contrasting
biological assemblage. Dung beetles, blanket

   crawlers.

Isolated from the web of complete human blood. It's not
just that we're different. It's that I picture burrowing

   scabies.

Lice. Mange lather on a brain-in-the-jar. Yes,
there is a trajectory: they face each other and

   shriek.

It lodges blue in my ear like a blowtorch flame. They're howling
downward, dropping: a retrograde transspecies. Tedious, trail

   diggers.

   Yet

      they are not
      alone on this
      small

         largely
         contaminated,
         gray planet:

>   there's a host,
>   tiring and foolish,
>
>   scatterlings at the gate.
>
> I feel them below me. Buck brained, dazed. Regulated,
> curfewed. Some sort of calibrated order: cross eared and floppy
>
>   eyed.
>
> Mome. Stubs. Tramping the dust. Though my anterior diagrams
> and plates are marinus, I do not witness my
>
>   origins.

Steve Fisher

hang over use in pharmacopia

(one)

—winter—

Cold bloated head
pulsing like a city borough
poor circulation
under the covers still
you get up
it's unreasonable, demanding—

hell-gnats swarm
the fornix & bodyslate:
throughout the apartment,
thrapping weather-split boards snarl and crack
a parallel condition in this poor hovel.
You notice darkness
outside
and wonder what it's all about.

At first footdown, oh fuck,
the usual rotating sickness
begins suddenly, starts
thick like horse skin
entombed in and out of vision and body.

   Bladder thumbtacks.
   Spinal tenement nerves, a carnival
   of sounds like sirens
   pressed through
   a squeegee—

once while shuddering you ring
as if constructed from bone chime.

Rock Salt & Glissandos

You shake
like an idling engine
a concentration breaker —

   so the oven: nail
   yourself to the heat!
Get back the circulation
known a split-sick second ago
   of yesterday
then — knee down in prayer — locate
the pills just saved for this moment.

Take them.
Slowly work up
through the hours.
Get better, get off —

   any mop-rung
   drunk will tell you
   this sickness cure — D.T.s or not —
   is close to antibiotics and the clap:

   only from the clap
   you won't get high.
   but the illness will torch itself from you.

   Euphorically,
after mixing your tranques and soft
narcotics in your wedged gagging hang over
state, you notice this combo
warming the body, clearing the receptors
   up there
cutting your intake of smokes —

   you
tidy up noticeably
get your ass into the shower
pay the bills

Steve Fisher

even do the dishes and
find that
   you're *ready*.

Altering this hang over
for yourself
is like a grace spread entirely
over the world;
a nationality
un-bolting
strict with reason —

nerves as steady as
candle flame:

Latter hundred lbs head.
Hello sunshine,
really it's morning after all
of this.

Rock Salt & Glissandos

whorl

Another black, pasty morning shrouded the camp. And Nacho, like always, was up early, getting ready for his job as a porter in the library. I saw him with a can of Magic Shaving Powder. He shaved about every forth day, but the job was a daily thing, and at least twice a week the librarian threatened to write him up over his beard stubble. Usually with a guard present. Finally, he would shave. I never liked that aspect of working, either: just tighter confinement around the rules of prison, like a hat size that was constantly being reduced.

But I knew Nacho. He had lived across from me, in the dorm, for close to a year. One of the first things I had noticed were the two teardrops he had, green teardrops, tattooed below the corner of his left eye: each drop represented five years in stir. He also had a large cobra, coiled in the small of his back, that lifted up his spine to the slender area of his neck. His arms were designed with affiliation symbols, club symbols, and during the lock downs—when separated from his homeboys—we sometimes kicked it together. But since I wasn't working, I had Nacho get me up that morning for breakfast. He'd said that the school, across from the library, might be looking for another porter. The plan was to check it out with him after chow.

The rest of the dorm just snored contentedly, like apes stretched out in a tropical lull. I laid in bed scratching, not at all eager to work or to hustle up one of their jobs.

I knew that porters were a special type of janitor who hung out a lot on the job, after they cleaned and mopped and did the rest of their schedule. They were often contacts between yards, running a sort of messenger service for small favors: no room for scrubs in this line of work. But most of them *had* been fucked over at one time or another, say, by a twenty-year-old guard, fresh from the academy, who confused prison with the duties of a high school hall monitor. Yet Nacho had tried to school me, the previous night. He explained it this way:

"Capone, Atwood, all them old gangsters used to be porters. Now you have Crips and El Rukins, Bloods who are porters."

"Yeah?" I had told him.

"Shit," he said, "it's an honorable tradition, a *tough* tradition."

He then leaned a little closer:

"I heard that James Brown worked as a porter. The *God*father, *ése*. A real classy bro in the union."

I had told him all right, I might become a porter, but as usual I was thinking about my own ass. We were in a high-medium institution, and you got fucked around badly if you didn't hire on somewhere. They started by having you rake rocks, on the track by the dorms which enclosed our yard. Then, when you refused, they took an amount of "good time" and put you on the shotgun crew. When you told them to jam that crew you were taken off the yard, placed in a higher, super-maximum run, and given a cell with some head case. I knew there were plenty of nuts around *our* camp, and felt no need to be on a permanent, lock down basis with one. So I figured the sensible thing would be to cover myself, to just fart along with the game until I made a lower-security yard. And since jobs meant bosses and authority, I also thought it would be sensible to work as little as possible.

It was barely seven o'clock in the morning. Nacho came back wearing blue-striped boxers, scuffing the floor with his shower shoes. He dumped the shaving material on his bed and sat down. Opened his locker. I saw the roll on his stomach, and the old knife wound which glowed like cartilage upon his left side: someone had once caught him from behind on a third tier in the walls, some shit or the other about who had the claim to a job opening. I exhaled sawdust from the last of my cigarette, thinking of breakfast, peeling slowly, at first, from my sheets to get dressed. Our shirts were blue. The air was black. My rug was a towel I had folded under the bunk. And the dorm was freezing when you had hot, Arizona skin. I got into my clothes as quickly as possible, the light from the bathroom like a white frosting on my eyes. I glanced at Grissom, my cellmate, as I tied on my boots. He was alright. He just snored under the hairy, black blanket. Nacho still sat on his bed in his boxers, unfolding T-shirts, his television on. I tucked in my shirt and called him a cold, callused motherfucker. He put his teeth together and hissed at the wall.

"Five minutes," he said, adjusting the volume on his set. Always this nervous bit of fiddling.

"Alright," I told him, "but I need some air. I wanna breath air again."

"*Su aliento hule a mierda*," he said. "Your breath smells like shit."

"No doubt."

I put my jacket on and went outside, spitting at the trash can that stood near our walk. I glanced at the sky. The world up there was like an asphalt para-

Rock Salt & Glissandos

chute. Rugged, wet charcoal. The yard and the trailers looked worse, like filmed reports I'd seen of outback Nicaragua. The smarter convicts wore stocking caps, going into and coming out of the chow hall. I drifted, looking for my breath against the clouds. And porters went through this shit every morning? Nacho came out jacketless, wearing his shades. "*Fuck,*" he said. "*Cold* out here." But all he did was shrug. We footed it the short distance to the chow hall.

There was a short line when we arrived. We walked up the cattle ramp, which was built against the wall, hooking at the corner to the right. It was spacious, almost elevated in there, though a hundred steel tables were cemented in the floor. Each table was fitted with four attached stools, and glowed under these snarling, length-long fixtures of light. It was like looking at a train of fluorescent cigarettes up there, but the overall feeling — with the thirty-foot walls and the ticking echo, the rafter vents and the smell of blower fans — was that of being dropped into a huge, Styrofoam cup.

I leaned against the halfwall, looking in at the workers on the serving line, watching the pancakes cook behind them on the grill. No, that wasn't the job for me either. I still felt about four-inches numb and wanted, in particular, to listen to a woodwind quintet: it was *sound* that I needed, just a form to balance my rhythms against, but all I heard was an inmate up front who'd been shorted a container of milk . . . by one of the bluecap civilian employees: "I ever catch you out here," the inmate hollered, "I'll strip the bark from your ass!" There was a solid panel — no glass — above the serving window, so the bluecaps could have limited contact with us. They could pretend, for instance, that they were hiding behind trees. The inmate plowed along, out through the turnstile, but only with a partial tray.

"And don't forget my MILK, *ass*hole," Nacho yelled in when we stepped up to the window. He got his stuff, but I had to reach in, because the bluecap pulled my tray from the ledge and walked off. The guards just stood there, writing down names that they knew the faces belonged to.

"Later," said Nacho, looking across the room.

Some of his pardners were sitting upper-center in the chow hall, so I grabbed a table in the corner and agreed to meet him in the library. Breakfast was the time for fruit, cereal, for sugar. The little packets went into socks, pockets, up sleeves. Various bags were brought in for cereal, which were then crotched or otherwise handled. I took my banana and dropped it through the booster slit I'd cut in the lining of my jacket. A white guy, decades older than me, set his tray on the table. I sliced at my pancake with a small plastic spork. The old guy didn't say a thing.

One side of my pancake was tough. The other was mostly batter. It was like chewing a brown leaf that had been coated with paste. I dropped it from my mouth grotesquely to my tray.

"Who can stand to get out of bed for this shit?" I asked.

I caught this wild, emerald span of oval, when the old guy raised his eyes up to mine. His head was still bent.

"They know how to scam a pancake," he said. "You didn't really expect breakfast, did you?"

"Guess not," I said. "Not when they know we could eat a whole slaughterhouse."

"Took twenty years for me to choke one of these down," he said, sporking at the pancakes, "but less than a morning to regret it. Now I just stick to the cereal. You can eat it dry, when the milk's sour."

His head was still down. I splashed the milk on my flakes.

The chow hall guards, like those in the rest of the joint, thrived on this game of lower polarity. Their trick was to block your needs, *as they came up*, through personal interpretation of the policy manual: raw pancakes. Spoiled milk. It was strictly an authoritative game, based on the idea of depriving the residents. I didn't quite understand it, but one of the advantages to working in the kitchen was being able to prestep the bluecaps and the guards and to eat, regularly, before the food went bad. But I had long ago learned how to fast on tobacco.

I carried my tray up to the dish window, hungry, chewing some dry cereal. A green banana slid by on the floor. The guard I passed in the exit ramp said nothing, his chin pointy and angular, resembling a garden trowel. Outside, three other cops looked me over. A thin crack of light divided the sky, and I imagined being trapped under a black beetle's shell. I went back to the dorm and picked up my cap. Grissom was still sleeping, grinding his teeth, his arms stretched up like a forked branch.

Another black, pasty morning. They could go on forever, especially when you started out tweaked. And who really wanted to work an institutional shift, anyway? I snagged my cap, then walked out in to the dayroom.

The library and school were located outside the yard, on a restricted and fenced-off section of the camp. You needed a pass from the house cop to get up there. I tracked him down, got one, and headed across the yard. Other convicts, wearing orange jump suits, milled around the west perimeter, waiting for various crew bosses. I looked away from them, no way, and crunched along in the frozen Arizona mud. More residents hung around the South Administration, waiting to get in to see their counselors. Prison counselors were supposed to help you get paperwork and so forth to places like the parole board and the classification committee, though I never saw an enthusiastic-looking face over there. But the turnstile I needed was just off to their left, below one of the gun towers. I dropped my pass into the slot. The guard pulled it in, examining me. She looked down at my boots, yelling through the glass.

"Lift your feet!" she hollered.

I showed her my brogans.

"Go!"

She pushed the button and I rolled the gate open. I passed through and

Rock Salt & Glissandos

closed it, watching a cop patrol the North Visitation Center. Three fences beyond me lay five other yards, including a minimum and a drunk driving facility: cash yards, the way Nacho had it figured. I walked along, past visitation, past another locked fence at the edge of the school. I stopped between the school and the library. A sort of divider terrace was cemented between buildings, where a few students hung out, smoking. I glanced through the school window, into the office where the secretary worked: just a short blonde in a loose red skirt, cafeteria plump, talking on the phone. Probably to a cop. Definitely not worth getting out of bed for, every day. I grabbed open the door on the library.

Officially the library was still closed. Nacho and one of his homeboys were sitting at a far table, near one of the few walls that held books, smoking, drinking coffee, bullshitting. The parole board, to my left, was locked. So was the office, on my right. And they were building another wall, an inner door, just in front of where I stood, though nobody was working on it at the moment. The library hung gray with outside light, light that drifted in through the rectangular, back window. Next to Nacho stood an industrial-sized vacuum cleaner. The guards weren't around.

I walked on the thin carpeting, just as Nacho rose for another coffee.

"C'mon, he said. "I'll fix you up."

"You know I don't fix with that shit," I told him.

"Might as well, until Busch gets here. There's milk, *ése*."

We hopped over the check-out counter and went into a large room behind the magazine stand. The room had a series of locked wooden cabinets, and a small window that overlooked the yard. It was cold in there and I felt lost, like a tiny bug on a dark blanket. Nacho opened one of the cabinets with a key, then whipped out a full pot of coffee he had stashed. I suddenly remembered who Busch was, as Nacho poured us a round.

"Ain't Busch the one who had the top of his ear sawed off with a comb?" I asked.

Nacho's eye's slickened with coffee oil, like he was laughing at a private joke.

"Don't have to let it bother you," he said in his light, Spanish accent. "You can just mop up. Take care of other business."

"Jesus Christ, Nacho. I thought you were my friend."

"Just don't pay any attention to him, that's all."

He handed me a cup with fold-out paper handles. I sipped at the coffee, yawning, certain that the gray dawn was likewise smogging my head.

The reason they had squared Busch's ear off had to do with his thing about queers: he had only a Christian understanding of homosexuality, was loose in the head, and—on top of that—wasn't sure whether he was knickknack or not. He'd walk up to people and start in on this line about dick sucking. Very quiet-like, as in perverse, and usually about someone they knew: "I know why your buddy got rolled up," he'd say. "They caught him in the supply closet, sucking dick. You oughta be careful, 'cause he's come on to me. He's as queer as they come, man, and I just wanted to warn you that he's always ready to give head." He would then stare at you with puffed cheeks, forearms extended, the right side of his sunglasses balanced on top of that squared-off ear. Next time, in a group, he'd be speaking about the Lord. And how you can be SAVED IN PRISON if you attend the Bible studies which are offered in the Chapel. A lot of people with strange ideas hid in that Chapel, but with Busch, and as he spoke, you felt he'd want to jack you off with a handful of Bible ink. I just couldn't picture *my*self, alone, in a schoolroom with him, dipping rags in the same bucket and washing down the chalkboards. And besides, I liked women: they sometimes said funny things when they got hungry, and to me they tasted a lot better.

I took a serious step back from Nacho.

"Listen, they should have put that guy in the dribble unit a long time ago. How am I supposed to work with a fruit basket?"

Nacho laughed.

"Sadistic motherfucker," I told him, but I also laughed a little. I was getting a short wire from the coffee.

"A job around here is a job," he said, as we headed back to the counter. "A-sides, you're the one who asked me about it."

"But you're the one who *sold* me on it. Just what the hell were you thinking about?"

We hopped over the counter. Nacho said, "I was thinking if you got the job, we could run him off. Only reason I haven't's 'cause it's an Anglo job over there. And it's a good one, 'cause it starts at fifteen cents an hour. Plus benefits, *ése*."

"But you know I'm not gonna step on anyone's shit unless they crowd me, even his," I said. "Now what?"

Nacho sat down and kicked his feet up on the table. His homeboy only grinned.

"Easy. Fuck Busch. Fuck the crew. Just work the job your own way."

It's what I would figure, but I knew that these things seldom worked out. Nacho said something in Spanish to his pardner. They nodded at each other.

"Know who was working here when I started? Little Sulfur Scottie. *There* was a case for you."

"Oh, yeah," I agreed, and then thought: every show in this camp is like pulling roots from someone's head: there's always a state of *pre-existence* to transform, in order to get *your* shit out of the old headlocks. You either did it, or punked-out. I squatted against the wall, looking off into the law library. "Alright," I told Nacho, "who's the cop that does the hiring around here? I'll check it out with him."

"I hear ya," he said. "Just go over to the school and look around. I think his name's Colon."

"Officer Colon?"

Rock Salt & Glissandos

"Shit *yeah*," said Nacho. Even his pardner was laughing.

"Fuck an A," I said. Officer Colon. The perfect man for the job.

I set my coffee down and walked to the door just as two residents wearing tool belts swaggered in. Another carried the electric drill. They stopped at that inner door frame, ready to bolt up the wall. It looked like a loud project, deafening. Then I saw Big Ed, outside. He was leaning against the school. I went over and he told me he'd seen Officer Colon around.

I walked in and got a drink from the fountain. The school was just a corridor with six rooms on either side, most of the rooms now filled with students. I could hear the tin of programmed music, softly from the office, but the classroom doors were closed so it was fairly calm, fairly quiet in there. I stood at the bulletin board as a door cracked open down the hall. A cop with a square cap looked out, almost as if he were hiding from someone. It was usually the other way around. I made a slight move, turning my head from the board. The face was as shiny as a summer squash.

"Hey, Colon."

He had large eyeball sockets, and his pupils floated as they rolled over to mine. It really looked like he'd been drinking from a two-dollar bottle. He just gazed at me, holding the door against his shoulder.

"Understand you need a porter," I said.

"We can talk in here," he said, pushing the door open. I walked over to the door.

Colon was standing in the center of a small windowless room, which had been converted into an office: institutional books, a calendar on the wall, stuffy. Next to the typewriter sat a stack of incident reports, still blank, just waiting to be filled out. It looked like a trap to me. Colon adjusted his cap, assuming this very superficial tone.

"So, you'd like to be a porter," he said. "I'm not in the habit of hiring just anyone."

I thought of Busch, putting his statement to terms right away. I looked him over in the low, pulsing light.

"I'm not in the habit of working just anywhere."

Colon wasn't that tall, but his head tapered in. Ears, Christ, pointing out like rudders. His nose cast a shadow, a triangle, on the right side of his cheek, and with the fluorescence humming down he seemed to whorl before me like a cigar tube.

"What makes you think you can cut it as a porter?" he asked

"I know I'll work hard for my store money," I lied.

"Tell you what," he said, in a lingering boxed accent. "You go over to South Admin and put your name on the list for education porters. You come back this afternoon, after I've had a chance to think it over. We can then discuss you as an applicant."

"Fine," I told him. "I'll get right over to that list."

I looked at him in the room and, as I left, decided against the whole thing.

157

Steve Fisher

I'd really only been trying to get out of the morning, but with just a squint of the Colon (and fueled by the yee-haw of the bluecaps in the chow hall) I took it further than any cubic, state lives: prison, I realized, could be approached as a sort of museum of the reductive: you consistently found people who could do nothing more than meddle with you, simply because they were small. Colon, Busch, tower guards, bluecaps: all became *exhibits*, to me, of people with lower instinct, of people whose lives fed on a need to reduce and constrain. I'd need an appointment to get into South Admin and sign on the book. It could take months, and I'd have to push *more cops*, including my counselor, to arrange it. Colon, apparently, assumed he could just spin me in all directions, but I now had the high angle and it helped distance me from their worlds: they all led a fractional existence, a melon slice, deathly.

The door closed behind me. Colon was on the other side. I relaxed in the hallway, the canals in my head flowing warmly with blood. I saw Nacho outside with a rag and some glass cleaner. I lit up a rollie, walked over.

"What up?" he said, turning back to the window. I liked the way that sounded.

"Colon wanted to take me down through it," I told him, "So I left him in that little closet they use. He's in there with the Book of Mormon, waiting on Busch."

"I just barely thought of something else," said Nacho. "You might be able to work out of maintenance."

"I'm not cut out to build walls."

I pivoted, just as the secretary came from the school. She was running a handful of papers across the terrace, very official, very red in that skirt, too important to even look in our direction. But fortunately my thinking had a wind of solar flare and I woke up, remembering who I was. Remembering something that could solve my whole problem. I watched as she walked along.

"You have an office clerk named Mango?" I asked.

She stopped, clutching the papers in her chest. I'd only known Mango a short while.

"Jeffery Mango? Wears glasses?" she asked.

"Yeah. What kind of hours you have him on?"

"Is there something I can help you with?"

"Not really," I said. "This is more of an academic matter."

"He's here in the afternoon, usually no later than one."

"Thanks," I told her. She opened the door to the library. It sounded like auto shop in there, with all the drilling, the hammering going on. Nacho put his rag to the window, looking in after her.

"*Culo pacoso*," he said.

"All right," I told him, "I've got an idea. No more of this portering shit. No more brownsuits, bluecaps, and especially those gray legs, over in maintenance. The bastards only trick bag a motherfucker."

Rock Salt & Glissandos

"You're gonna *max* out," Nacho said enthusiastically.
"I'm gonna sleep in, if I'm lucky," I said. Nacho stepped out of the way.
"How's this window look from back there?"
I looked it over. It was as clear and clean as fifty-million FM watts, though it really didn't interest me.
"Really tits," I told him. "Don't fall in."
Nacho pulled a cigarette from behind his ear, looking proudly at his work. I walked out of there, through the turnstile, past South Admin and the line waiting outside. I wanted to separate from authority as much as possible, hopefully using Mango as my blade. My idea, his execution, something like completing a musical phrase. I looked to the south, to the mountains in Mexico. It was still grisly, tar-like up there, the sky loaded with thick, Mexican clouds. I walked back to the dorm raw throated, thirsty for salad. I entered my cube. Pulled down a book. Settled out on my bunk. But my bunk, as usual, was like lying in the cup of a plow. I opened to a page, glancing at Grissom. He just snorted and rolled over, like a drugged beast that was chained to the wall. Who the fuck wanted to porter under the obligation of grief? I aimed my lamp on the book and opened to a page.

"Wake up man, chow. They're gonna close in fifteen minutes."
"Go burn the warden's dog."
"C'mon Holmes, they're serving cheeseburgers."
Grissom tapped on the tubing of my bunk. It hollowed out in my head.
"You're a *hen*roid, Grissom!"
"What's a 'henroid'?"
"*You're* a henroid," I said.
"Well, I'm telling you. It's almost one o'clock."
"Alright . . ."
Grissom was only a youngster, but we got along. He'd done his work one day with an ice pick, after a therapy session with his court-appointed counselor. He was then issued to me by the state.
I put my feet on the floor and locked up my rack.
"Cheeseburgers, huh?"
"Yeah," said Grissom, "let's scarf."
"Sure," I said, standing up. We headed through the dorm. I didn't see Nacho around.
"And before you ask," said Grissom, "neither of us got any fucking mail."
"Yeah."
The day room and guard's cage were dark, but a slit of light shone from the doorjamb. I was ready for the yard. Grissom and I stepped out, into a tremendous chrome October, the sun a horn of silver-blue embroidery. It was hot. I felt like an isolated, solar being. The call over the yard barker said the hall would close in ten minutes but we made it inside, into the line. When we moved in front of the serving cage, Grissom knocked on the glass.

His roaddog was in charge of putting the burgers on our trays. He gave a nod and Grissom laid two fingers, very casually, against the window pane. The dog looked at me, counted the trays in front of us, feeling around for the cops. There was one at the serving window, along with a bluecap whose lips had caked like a dried cheese. Others drifted behind the bluecap, but no one looked over his shoulder.

We moved along.

Grissom's roaddog pressed two hamburgers apiece on our trays, passing them quickly to his pardner on the left. The pardner had the lettuce. He reacted coolly, though scrambled, stretching the lettuce across the burgers into a natural, resilient, form-fitting leaf dome. As my tray slid down I walked forward, watching it through the glass. The bluecap pushed it out and I grabbed it, then walked into the center of the chow hall. Grissom's roaddog had risked a thirty-day lock down, but the risk was minimal because the dog knew his art. The afternoon was already looking better than the morning.

I ate quickly with Grissom. He told me the story of a female cop who had inflated a basketball the previous night in recreation, where he was employed, but I didn't want to hustle work there either. Grissom sort of jutted his whole upper body as he spoke, like he was walled-in to a speed-metal soundtrack. I gave him my cookies right before I left, knowing that he got off on the sugar. The same cops working breakfast were again standing at the door, and as they looked me over I thought of them in their tiny, fractional head tombs. What a way to die, death! I got away from them, fast, and onto the yard.

It was a little after one when I got back to the school. Education, like the yard, was now jammed with inmates, but the library was also open. I saw Nacho leaning shirtless against the fence, collecting cigarettes from two people I didn't know. Benefits. Then Mango came from the school, looking pissed. He took long strides with his short legs, ripping the library door open. I got a smoke from Nacho, waited five minutes or so until Mango came back. This time, he strolled.

"Mango," I said.

He looked over. We crossed to the dirt by the fence. Even with good posture he only came up to my chin.

"You're another that looks satisfied," he said. "Or did I confuse that with disgusted? What's new?"

"I should be asking. You sure looked hot a minute ago."

He looked sharply toward the school, then up at the yard. His brown hair was blowing in the afternoon wind. Beyond him lay miles and miles of unwanted state desert. He gazed back, toward the school.

"The cop in here complained to the secretary that someone got a grade because I did their work," he said. "Can you imagine that? The students take the tests, not me, but this idiot Colon thinks he's busted a conspiracy because I helped someone solve a problem. My boss doesn't care but I do, only because he's harassing me. And it's not even his job. We hate each others', guts."

"Yeah?"

"Yeah," he said, looking into my eyes. "We got into it another time, over pretty much the same thing."

"What happened?"

"I told him to eat shit with tacks through his tongue. I wanted to offend him for being such a punk."

Someone opened the door to the library, and I again heard the *plomb plomb plomb* of inmate construction. What shit.

"He's only a *fraction*," I told Mango, "not a total human being. His thoughts on everything are governed by a fucking state handbook. Makes for some strange reactions."

Mango put his hands on his hips, making small circles in the dirt with his feet.

"A state fraction," he said. "Kinda funny, when you think about it like that. Still, too bad he's gotta work up here."

"I figure he'll be working here no matter what. The next one to come along is pretty much the same formula."

"Yeah," he agreed.

"The exceptions seem to hang back a little, but I'm sure as hell not finding many. That's why I need a favor."

"Let's make it quick," said Mango. "I've got to get back before class starts."

I noticed Colon at the door, staring out the window at us. Even here, the fucker wanted in. I turned my back to him.

"Register me for drafting," I said. "Just put it on the computer, so I won't get in any jams when classification looks through my file."

"You want to cut away from this yard, huh?"

"You bet. Can you do it?"

"Sure," he said. "Tonight, after the shift change."

"Perfect. What am I gonna owe you?"

Mango reached in his shirt pocket, dug out a cassette.

"Know John Handle, over on your yard? Give this to him." He handed me the tape.

"Nothing to it," I said, and Mango, in his own way, simply walked off. That's all there was, no pulling of teeth.

Drafting.

In exchange for a porter-type favor.

The afternoon classes began, and Mango headed into school with everyone else. That left me and Nacho, and also his pardner, out on the terrace. But my ass was now covered, and I had no immediate plans. None, whatsoever. Nacho came over with a bag of Mexican hot chips, offering me a pull. I'd been down long enough that I thought my taste buds had turned to wax, but I nearly jumped from the spice when I chewed them. Nacho laughed. His homeboy laughed. We watched as an old flatbed work truck drove slowly along the perimeter, taking a load of convicts out to a crew site. They stood on the wooden platform holding a single rail, jump suits creased in the wind. Colon still looked out from the school: insulated, protected, mindless, dangerous.

I turned and walked off. I passed Busch on the walk and said nothing, leaving him and his ear to the regulations of Colon. Good pair, I thought, choosing *my* time, not theirs.

Which meant drafting. I knew it would keep me off the street in the mornings. And that was the only thing that mattered.

I cut lazily with the tape to John Handle's. Through the bright, nearly effortless, helium afternoon.

tightening the rings on the sun with my forehead

for George Crumb

This light, this sun. This music I listen to
on a tiny, blue earth. Over my Walkman headphones.

      This sound:

      these bells,
      these rods.
This metallic orchestration
foaming through my
skinyard.

This heliocentricity, this fire. The whole
static inner ear mutating particles to life

      through timbre:

      these pistons,
      water grips.
That burn neon sculpture through
      my head
crashing like white water
      against my skull.

This world in the crest of my bloodhive. These notes,
these lungs. Monatomic sprockets glistering in my

      brain sacs:

      birds are
      flocking,
though above me the sky
      is empty.

Steve Fisher

    I rise up

and rub foreheads with this heat. These melodies. These
flash pods clustered into bijou, interritorial. This head

    of mine:
      hollow
  like a domed arena
kick beating *kick* beating
   percussive words
   on a *largo* wave.

Far away from this receding, blue globe. This light,
this sun. This music radial, alert. From flesh to

    fire
  to the temple
of my cerebral lobes:

     I,
   ecstatic,
wearing headphones
    and
   listening
      s.
     d
    r
   a
  w
up

Rock Salt & Glissandos

ugly and multiple

I remember flying roaches ensnared my vision
like black swooping felt-tip fuckers,
thickening my step while I woke up ugly and multiple
to a sweating beer and fading light
no brighter than a courtesy lamp
in an old rambler

then got busted for felonious seizure and giving
the dept. the finger at a wind-up intersection
easily dominoed by a wheelchair stray

Was cuff-numb/booked; photo, fingerprinted and old techniqued,
and left to commune with the hard walls and empty air

I drank to be alone and now I'm finally not

Steve Fisher

such pittance, the thoughts

Drive this sado-worker

  —this
office-white poleneck barrel lip

  paper-hawkedfaced
  swivel-johnny
  form hustler

into the earth—

  Ridicule his presence!

  Heckel his meditations!

  Deny his post!

  Kneecap before mercy!

  —a blasé
earth compound
such that animals
grace away from . . .

blockades

"Crestfallen," for example: one shouldn't linger, or *stop* at that feeling, nor descend into pity and sorrow of the repressed heart. That's too easy, and obviously the reaction most people indulge in, because it leads to emptiness: the emptying of being crestfallen. Or, to exemplify it in other terms, allows for that dull death—or sleep, if one is so lucky—people truly desire, especially if riffed, over and over, time and again, with such blockades a peaceful heart and anatomy has withheld from them. The only solution I instruct myself in, at such times, is to grapple—to crash and bang among thought and words—against that provocation until it is no longer an intrusion, but a settled account, lifted away from the "souring along the vines." Swelling and bruises dissolve in time, but it doesn't leave me ten-counted on the mat. Sad, disturbed at moments . . . by pulling the pin and counter attacking, I'm allowing myself—should it arrive—a district free of that dull death. To collapse is to offer nothing, and though nothingness has its range of benefits and applications, in this "crestfallen" context: collapsing dims the ventricles, stimulates translucency, and plugs your ears with candle wax just as the band begins. The error is to linger. The solution is to accommodate disturbing events with raw reactions.

Steve Fisher

Stephen James Fisher was born in Ohio and grew up in Michigan, where his father worked for Ford Motors. Entering his teens in the late sixties, at the height of the psychedelic era, he experimented with alcohol and various drugs—and soon became a heavy user of both.

After getting a GED, he attended a music college in Boston, where he learned his trade, piano tuning—at which he excelled. According to his companion (and now his literary executor), Cherry Vasconcellos, "Steve valued little in the material world. He owned a pair of black Reeboks, two pairs of Levis, some shirts. His books were the exception. He had a large, pristine collection, worth some money. He bought, sold, and traded with other collectors. He collected Charles Bukowski, Harry Crews, Knut Hamson and others—and a complete run of Nelson Algren."

"He refused to enter any kind of rehab program. At least once he was offered a drug program as an alternative to going to prison and he chose serving time. He was convicted and sent to Arizona State Prison."

"The two years before his death were probably the best of his life. He was free. He'd written a lot in prison and had stories in *TriQuarterly*, *Shenandoah*, *Epoch*, *Iowa Review* and other magazines. He'd finished a screenplay that was getting attention from the Director's Guild. He'd fallen in love. Then he moved to Los Angeles, where, in the course of a year, he slid back into narcotics addition. Then one Sunday he drove back to Tucson, where, a week later—on February 7, 1993—he injected a massive combination of cocaine and heroin which he knew would end his life. He was thirty-seven."